Improve Your Teaching

Written by Mike Rathbone

Published by Scholastic Publications Ltd,
Marlborough House, Holly Walk,
Leamington Spa, Warwickshire, CV32 4LS

Written by Mike Rathbone
Edited by Janet Fisher and
Jackie Cunningham-Craig
Sub-edited by Jane Morgan
Illustrated by Helen Herbert
Designed by Sue Limb

Typeset by Studio Photoset, Leicester
Printed and bound by Richard Clay Ltd,
Chichester, Sussex

ISBN 0 590 70948 8
Front and back cover designed by Sue Limb

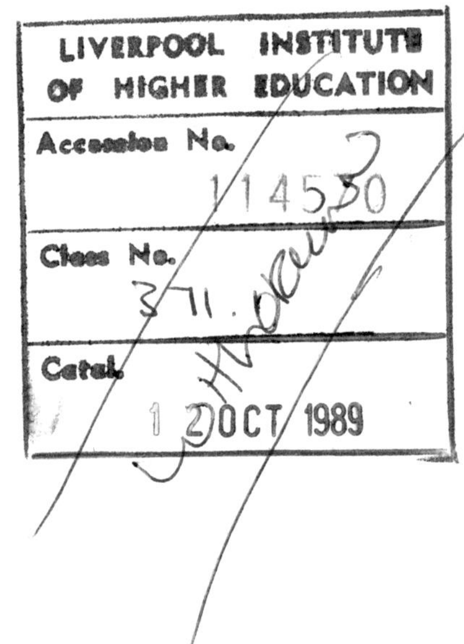

Contents

Introduction

The complexities of the job

When teachers are talking about themselves and their jobs the phrase 'chalk face workers' is often used to refer to the teachers who are actually teaching children in the classroom throughout the school day. This popular description distinguishes class teachers from colleagues who have left the classroom to become headteachers or teacher trainers etc. Although most former 'chalk face' teachers try to spend at least some of their working week in classrooms, the label is clearly quite a useful way of describing the 'front line' position of classteachers in schools. However, it is equally clear that such a description does not come anywhere near to indicating the variety and complexity of the tasks which primary teachers are expected to perform. Teachers are *in loco parentis*, responsible for the safety of perhaps 35 children, and for teaching them to become proficient in various aspects of the curriculum, from language and mathematics to social skills and physical and aesthetic activities.

Teachers must encourage children to learn about people and places, to think about moral values and world religions, and to consider issues related to health and hygiene. They must keep records of each individual child's progress, recognising the need for extra help where necessary for outside advice and assistance.

Behavioural problems of increasing variety and complexity have to be faced.

In some instances these reflect the problems of society as a whole. Drugs, hooliganism, and child abuse, are obvious examples, to which fears about the transmission of AIDS have recently been added.

In addition teachers often take children away on educational visits, frequently in their own 'holiday' time, and sometimes at considerable financial cost to themselves. The implications of recent disasters during such visits are still being felt. They have brought home to teachers the grave implications of taking responsibility for such trips.

Primary teachers also spend weekends and evenings, fund raising, not only to buy educational 'extras', but also many basic items such as books, papers and computers.

In many classrooms, teachers are expected to work with children who are vastly different in ability, at different stages in their development, and of different ages. It is often expected that parents should be involved in the classroom too.

Sometimes teaching is carried out in conditions which are far from ideal and in many instances are getting worse. Money for resources is apparently getting less, and support services are being curtailed.

Yet demands upon teachers are likely to increase. The Education Reform Bill involves changes which will have significant implications for the running of schools (see Chapter 4). Teachers must keep themselves up to date with recent developments in CDT and information technology. They must accept the insistant clamour for appraisal. Sometimes these demands are met by attending courses at their own expense, usually out of school time.

At school, curriculum initiatives have to be considered and implemented. The newly evolved national curriculum will have to be taken into account. Recommendations from groups such as the Task Group on Assessment and Testing, and the Kingman Report on the Teaching of English, need to be considered. At home, books have to be marked and lessons prepared.

Of course, when students decide to make a career of teaching they ought to be aware of the demands of the job. If they are not then teaching practices soon demonstrate what is required.

For committed teachers, the endless complexity and variety of teaching, and the consistant interaction with children and with equally committed colleagues, are the things which give them greatest satisfaction in their work. Indeed this satisfaction, and the sheer enjoyment of working with enthusiastic, lively youngsters, has for years been the most significant reward for teachers as the status of the job has declined. Successive governments and ministers of education have appeared intent upon reducing the morale of teachers in schools. The salary scales reflect their low status. Compared with teachers in most European countries, classroom teachers in the UK are badly paid and are expected to participate in out of school activities, which their European counterparts have never had to worry about. The pay 'negotiations' of 1987 and 1988, which concluded with imposed settlements, show how important education is as a political issue, and also how poorly regarded teachers are as professionals. Teachers have been given conditions of service which say much about what they must do, but little about important aspects of teaching such as class size, time allowances for marking, and non-contract hours for teachers in primary schools.

In spite of all the difficulties associated with teaching however, and the complaints of some politicians and the media about falling standards in our primary schools, the overwhelming consensus of opinion is that primary education in the UK is of a high standard. One reason for this has been the continuing desire of most primary teachers to improve their practice and to develop further skills as teachers. Teachers coming into the profession, and teachers with comparatively short experience, are particularly enthusiastic about INSET, and ready to consider ideas to improve their classroom work.

This book sets out to make suggestions which teachers can consider when reflecting upon some aspects of their work. Though the suggestions have their foundations in some of the research which has been carried out in recent years on primary education, they are tempered by the experiences of teachers in primary schools.

Many important aspects have had to be left out, for just as the job of the primary teacher is vast, so would be the volume that sought to discuss every aspect of that job. Two things, however, require particular emphasis — evaluation and relationships.

Evaluation

When reading the book, it is hoped that teachers will be reflective about their own practices in the classroom. One of the most important characteristics of the effective teacher is an ability to think through situations and to develop strategies which apply to particular circumstances or children — to evaluate the processes of education as they are occuring in the classroom, and to determine how they might be changed to best serve the children.

Generally of course, the classroom is not the place where teachers can easily stand back and reflect on what they are actually doing. Research has frequently shown that teachers are surprised by

what they say and do in the classroom. Their perception of what is happening is clouded by the ever present need to talk to the children, to answer questions, and simply to be present in the classroom for the whole of every teaching day. This is particularly true of new teachers, and teachers in especially trying circumstances. They have great difficulty in carrying out an evaluation of their work, because of the pressures of their situations.

Probationary teachers and teachers in difficult situations need more opportunity than others to evaluate their teaching as they attempt to improve their skills.

Although teacher training courses do try to teach students the skills of evaluation and reflection, teaching practice for the student teacher cannot give a true picture of the work of a full-time teacher. Teaching practices come to an end, and students never actually have the total responsibility that class teachers have. Evaluation skills can therefore never be fully tested whilst the teacher is still training.

In the first year of teaching when the full pressures of class responsibility are felt and problems arise in the classroom, there is always the temptation to find solutions from a typical list of 'tips for teachers'. Experienced teachers in difficult circumstances may also seek such solutions. Grasping after straws in this way is typical of superficial classroom evaluation, and concentrates on symptoms rather than causes. An 'in depth' analysis of the situation is usually required, including the nature of the relationship between children and teacher and the organisation and management of the classroom.

As an example, let us suppose that discipline problems arise during a story-time session and that some children cannot answer questions about the story. Perhaps the teacher has not prepared well enough for the lesson or maybe the children are new to school and are not used to having stories read to them at home. Problems might also have been caused by children being distracted by their friends; they may have been sitting in uncomfortable positions on the floor, or in places where they could not all see the teacher.

In such circumstances it is far better to change the organisation of the classroom and/or the timetable, rather than increase the level of control. Even a change of book, perhaps the most obvious possible 'solution', may not necessarily be helpful in this situation.

Relationships

Establishing good relationships in a school and class is another key feature of a teacher's job. Every teacher, however experienced, has to build up relationships with a new class, and with staff in a school. Children quickly develop an impression of their teacher, and test it out in their early dealings with their teacher. They ask implicit questions.

How does their teacher respond to good work, to bad behaviour, to children who need extra attention, to the various aspects of the curriculum, to provocative situations?

If a good rapport between child and adult is established it can lead not only to a secure and necessary foundation for the child's education but also to a satisfying and stable period of teaching for the teacher. On the other hand, though most children are not by nature malicious, a lack of rapport between teacher and class can lead to disrespect for the teacher and ultimately to disruption in the classroom.

Staff in schools also question their colleagues. Is the teacher always co-operative and enthusiastic, or keen on some curriculum areas but not on others? Is the teacher able to cope with the demands of the job in all circumstances, or only in some? Is the teacher able to give and receive advice and help?

These are all points which concern the relationships which develop in a school. The way in which they are worked out creates that atmosphere which is so noticeable to anyone who visits the school.

Neither 'evaluation' nor 'relationships' are chapter headings in this book, for they are the twin strands that run through it from start to finish. Readers should consider what each section says implicitly about these two aspects, for they are central to the continuing development of effective primary school teaching.

Chapter One

Teachers and teaching

Visitors to schools, either experienced teachers or people who rarely go into schools, can usually see clear differences between the reception and upper primary classes. These are not only evident in the subjects being taught, but in the subject matter and in the teaching and learning methods used. Teachers working with different age groups may have different aims and philosophies. The opinions and dictates of headteachers, parents, local authorities, and the political party in power, also influence what happens in the classroom.

It is clearly not sensible to try to teach five-year-olds in the same way as eleven-year-olds are taught. The attention span of children increases as they get older, they are able to handle more advanced concepts and are more dextrous. They have wider interests, and are more self-reliant. Equally important is the fact that older children are moving towards the stage where they will leave the primary school.

Secondary or middle schools are likely to have more formal approaches to teaching than primary schools, although some middle schools are similar to primary schools in the first two years before the children move to the secondary-orientated upper forms. Older primary children need to be prepared for this more formal system, and so upper junior classrooms are usually more formal than those further down the school. The curriculum organisation and content are similar to those of the local secondary school, especially if there is genuine liaison between the primary and secondary schools.

During the early years of primary school, teachers aim as much to socialise the children as to develop their learning abilities. With good classroom practice and planning both of these aims can be attempted in an informal, though not unstructured, system of classroom organisation. Teachers encourage children to co-operate by splitting them into groups, to take part in informal play activities with, for example, sand, water and bricks. This play encourages experimentation and hence learning. This type of learning through play, together with input from the teacher, is a central feature of early education. Unfortunately its continuing relevance is frequently forgotten in later junior years.

During much of the infant's day, curriculum boundaries disappear as different themes are pursued. The children may make collages, attempt simple poems, paint and draw.

Children are often grouped together. This has to be done sensitively, and can be carried out in a variety of ways, as we will see in Chapter 2. Some methods of grouping are specifically aimed at making children more sociable. In a vertically grouped school, children of different ages are deliberately put together in one class, and put into mixed aged groups within the class. The older children are expected to help the younger pupils, not just in practical ways, but also with curriculum work.

This kind of socialisation occurs naturally as pupils co-operate, provided that the pupils are carefully chosen by the teacher. If the groups do not get on well, then not only will the classroom atmosphere be disturbed, but the children's intellectual development will suffer.

Control

Concern about control in the classroom is one of the major pre-occupations of teachers. Careful organisation will help a teacher to keep control in most classroom situations.

For example, the watching of a television programme can easily be disrupted if the teacher cannot see all the children or because the television area is cramped, or because the programme is too long for the children's attention span.

In PE lessons, if the apparatus is not easily available, or has to be 'dug out' from below stacks of chairs, children will become bored and consequently irritable.

Where there are problems of control, attempts must be made to discover the underlying causes. In the meantime, however, interim steps may have to be taken in order to continue the lesson. These may be sanctions or rewards, including reprimands of various kinds, incentives to do well, and removal of privileges such as break-times. Depriving children of a privilege like break-times also affects the teacher as children 'kept in' have to be supervised. In extreme cases children may be sent to the headteacher. Resorting to an external authority figure, however, does not mean that the teacher has in any way improved the relationship with the child; removal will not help avoid further disruption.

For teachers who have control problems it is frustrating to see that in classrooms which have good control there are often no obvious signs of how it is being maintained.

Consistent good behaviour stems from the ethos of a school. Where there is normally a good deal of purposeful, constructive activity discipline problems are less evident than in schools where for reasons of low morale in staff or pupils the whole exercise of schooling has apparently lost its purpose. By motivating children to learn we are also helping to maintain discipline.

Developing responsibility and self discipline in pupils is one of the major social aims of the school. To help with self-discipline, most schools have a fairly straightforward set of school rules, which are limited in number, and are designed primarily to ensure safety of pupils and staff. 'No running in the corridors' is an example.

A few schools, however, have other rules which do not have the specific purposes outlined above, neither do they reflect a rule system of the world outside school. Rules to do with the wearing of school uniform are such examples. Though the insistence on wearing school uniform may have very sensible and practical underlying reasons, trying to

enforce it may have a detrimental effect on the school as a whole, especially if some staff and parents are not convinced of its value. A member of staff who has control problems and tries to apply this type of role may increase those problems.

For the class teacher, especially newly qualified, school notes ought to include information on the general standards of discipline expected in the school. In the classroom, the teacher should try to apply broadly the same rules as his or her colleagues. Children have a very keen sense of justice, so that variations between teachers in the application of rules can make pupils uncertain and resentful.

Within the classroom a teacher must obviously act as fairly as possible in matters of discipline, and at least in the early days with considerable firmness. An initial firm approach is likely to eliminate the possibility of control problems later on. In many instances a lax approach to discipline by a new teacher, no matter how experienced, is interpreted by children as an invitation to do as they please. Once this idea has taken hold, it is extremely difficult for a teacher to re-establish control.

How then can the issue of control be approached by a teacher? Here is a list of ideas to consider:

Do

- Prepare lessons thoroughly. Know what the children should do next, when they have finished one piece of work. Keep apparatus and equipment to hand, with some pencils, rubbers etc available. Place equipment so that it is easily accessible to the children who need it.
- Wait for quiet before talking to the whole class.
- Catch a child's eye or direct a question at a child to bring that individual's attention back to the task in hand.
- Walk around the class, and when talking to individuals, ensure that you can see the rest of the class.
- Use positive, favourable comments when possible.
- Ask advice from experienced colleagues.

Don't

- Use sanctions which devalue subject areas, and suggest that some subjects can never be enjoyed. For example, don't stop a child doing games, or use extra maths as a punishment.

- Remove children from the room unless it is absolutely necessary.
- Be sarcastic when reprimanding children, or in commenting upon their work.
- Get into a confrontation situation with a child which will be seen by the class as a test of credibility.
- Lose your temper.

The real answer to control in the classroom lies in the mutual confidence and trust of pupils and teachers. Bad behaviour amongst pupils usually has several causes, and though sometimes the most significant factors are concerned with the school, teacher and class, often the reasons lie outside the school. The home background, peer group etc can all be contributory factors. If, in the teacher's opinion, the disruptive behaviour of one child is significantly influencing the other pupils, advice must be sought from the headteacher about possible referral to the educational psychologist. This should be done before the teacher has had to undergo too many traumatic experiences.

Unfortunately, with cut-backs in so many educational support services in local authorities, some schools have to continue to serve the needs of even the most disturbed children in the normal class situation.

In these cases the support of all staff, especially the most experienced, is necessary. Whatever means are used to try to help the situation, you should not ignore the insights and help which may come from parents. Try to meet with them and discuss the problems, if at all possible.

Communication skills

All teachers attach great importance to the socialisation of the children. It is part of the development of classroom relationships. Communication skills play a large role in forming these relationships as well as in helping the day to day routines of the classroom. The development of children's communication skills constitutes a large part of the language curriculum of schools, and often reflects the cognitive development of children.

Every teacher has to pass on knowledge and information to pupils, as well as instructions which enable children to use tools safely, carry messages, go through learning processes themselves etc. In doing this, the teacher has to consider many factors concerned with the child, the environment, and the reason for the communication.

Children cannot receive information properly if they are hard of hearing or have eye trouble. Expert advice is required, though teachers can help by positioning children carefully in the classroom. However, the support services which diagnose such problems very early in the child's school life are not resourced adequately enough to identify every child who needs help. Consequently the teacher has to be particularly observant, looking for the child who seems bored, cannot repeat what has been said, or cannot cope with what is on the board etc. Since these features can be observed in almost any child at some time or other, the chance of overlooking the child with a slight hearing or sight defect is great. An added complication is that children with common colds and coughs often have the same symptoms.

Even if all the children in the class have good hearing and eye-sight there are numerous other communication features which the teacher must be aware of.

The teacher needs to remember that:

- Nervous or agitated teachers (or indeed speakers of any kind) often speak too quickly, especially to children who have learning difficulties. Speech delivered more slowly than normal is understood and remembered more efficiently.
- Environmental factors can be quite distracting to listeners. This not only applies to the bus passing outside, but to the temperature of the classroom, and emotional events which occur to children. Some of these distractions can be eliminated. Those emotional upheavals which a child feels too sensitive to mention can be discovered by talking to children, and possibly parents, on an informal basis, for example at the beginning or end of the day.
- Large chunks of information are often only partly received and understood by children. Teachers should ensure that oral information is broken down into small, meaningful parts and that children have practice in listening to and retaining spoken instructions. Games like 'O'Grady Says' and 'Simple Simon Says' are useful with very young children. Older children derive a great deal of pleasure from a game like 'Chinese Whispers'. The results can be rather unexpected, and a source of serious discussion as well as amusement.
- Some children are able to process pictorial information much more easily than symbolic information, particularly when they are very young. Images constructed from what they see are remembered more easily than verbal clues. As they grow up some children become better at handling verbal information than their peers. Bearing in mind that in schools much information is passed on by reading and speaking and that some cannot be communicated in any other way, it is no wonder that some children are better able to understand and assimilate 'school work' than others.
- Children who actively participate in their learning are more likely to retain what they learn. Chalk and talk is not usually a very good way of teaching. Active participation may involve practical work, but active participation in discussion and in finding out information is also important.

Obviously some material is best given to the class as slabs of information, and pupils simply do not have time to learn everything for themselves. Nevertheless children must have the opportunity to learn how to learn for themselves, and how best to use given information.

Language work which includes reading, writing, listening and talking is expected to develop children's communication skills. Although we are unable to look at any of these important features in detail, we must consider the skills of the teacher as a questioner and as an organiser of classroom activities. The major purpose of questioning, in the primary classroom, is to develop the children's skills as communicators, particularly through the spoken word, and to improve their cognitive development. As almost every parent will affirm, most children, though not all, have no problems in talking, but for teachers, it is the quality of what is said which is important.

Talk

There is continuing lively debate about how children learn to talk, and still a great deal of research to be done on the subject. It seems likely that children imitate to some degree the language which they hear around them, and they draw conclusions about the rules of that language. It is probable too, that the reinforcement of the listener's responses, and to a small degree, the corrections which adults make to the child's attempts at language, are significant factors in how a child learns language.

There is evidence to suggest that certain types of interaction between children and adults, at home and at school, are the most significant factors in enhancing a child's cognitive development.

In the classroom the teacher can help children to develop certain aspects of talk by intervening at appropriate times. Situations have to be set up which allow children to become interested and involved in activities which encourage them to talk. We will look at how to organise such situations later in the chapter.

Joan Tough attempted to categorise children's talk, and the fostering strategies which teachers could usefully employ, in a series of useful volumes, for example *Listening to Children Talking* (Ward Lock 1976). I would recommend this work, and the work of Gordon Wells in the Bristol University study *Language at Home and at School* (see, for example *Language, Learning and Education,* NFER 1985).

Put simply, the teacher's aims are to lead the children into conversations which entail thinking about the future and the past, which lead to prediction, imagination and logical reasoning.

Questioning

In addition to passing on information, teachers have to make their pupils think. One way of doing this is to develop discussion between teacher and pupils and between the pupils themselves. The discussion can start from careful questioning. The way the questions are put is critical. In examining questioning in their classrooms teachers ought to consider:

- Are the questions 'open' or 'closed'?

If a question is open, the child has the opportunity to offer different answers with perhaps many possibilities of arriving at an answer. There may, indeed, be no wrong answers. Such a question might lead into a discussion about emotional responses to a poem.

'What do you think that the writer felt when writing this piece?', could start an interesting discussion after the teacher has heard a child read.

Open questions enable the teacher and child to develop a conversation more easily than questions which require a right or a wrong answer. This kind of questioning has implications for 'inference' which we will discuss in a later chapter.

- Which pupils are answering questions?

It is not unusual for classroom observers to notice that teachers tend to question some pupils much more frequently than others. Obviously, certain pupils offer to answer questions more frequently than their peers, but teachers usually have a lesson plan in mind and a set of aims which they hope to achieve within the session. If part of the lesson depends on a series of questions and answers, then the teacher is bound to be tempted to question pupils whom they anticipate will give the required answers. Teachers bring certain

expectations to their classrooms which may be based on the pupils' dress, use of language and general behaviour. They may be derived from the teacher's knowledge of where the pupil lives, the teacher's experience of other members of the pupil's family etc and they may be reinforced by the teacher's experience of the pupil.

Although unpredictable answers may not be unwelcome, they do sometimes mean that the teacher has to decide whether to follow up an unexpected answer immediately, whether to ignore the answer, or whether to accept the answer and go back to the original line of thought later on. Only experience can tell the teacher what strategy is most appropriate at any particular time. However, the teacher should never ignore an answer, since such indifference by the teacher will ultimately lead to indifference by even the most highly-motivated pupils.

The expectations which teachers have about their pupils, no matter how ill-founded, are also significant because pupils tend to live up, or down to them. This develops into a self-perpetuating situation where those pupils who initially derive most benefit from question-and-answer sessions continue to gain increasing benefit. Those who are not initially expected to respond will have little chance to influence the teacher's opinion of them, and hence they continue to receive less attention than their peers.

Another reason why some pupils do not become involved in answering teacher's questions is that they have received negative responses from previous teachers. If the teacher asks only closed questions, and the pupil has given wrong answers which have provoked ridicule or sarcasm from either the teacher or fellow pupils, then that pupil will try to avoid answering questions for fear of being subjected to similar treatment again.

Pupils can become very clever at avoiding answering questions. If a teacher insists that a particular pupil answers a question, the pupil may hesitate, so that the teacher asks another pupil and keeps the continuity of the lesson flowing. Pupils sometimes say that they did not hear the question, hoping that the teacher will ask someone else. Or a pupil may give an obviously irrelevant answer, hoping to making other pupils laugh, and hence draw the teacher's attention away from himself.

This sort of behaviour may in fact conceal a child who is desperately lacking in confidence.

The most significant example of avoidance behavour, however, is an abusive response to the teacher's question. Indeed, unruly behaviour in the classroom may itself be a reaction by pupils to their own lack of confidence, perhaps triggered, or contributed to, by the way the teacher asks questions. If pupils are consistently made to feel inadequate in the classroom, they often respond by trying to assert themselves in ways that can make the situation difficult for the teacher.

Is the teacher dominating the question and answer session?

Pupils' reluctance to join in question and answer or discussion sessions with the teacher often occurs because the teacher dominates the sessions. Gordon Wells points this out in his book *Language, Learning and Education* (1985). He advocates sessions in which teachers encourage pupils to express aims, make plans, recognise problems, look for alternative solutions, use resources and evaluate outcomes.

- Is the teacher dictating the pupil's responses by giving non-verbal clues which point to correct, or appropriate answers?

Children are very quick to spot a teacher's tendency to indicate when a pupil is on the right track. For example,
— some teachers pick up their chalk, or half turn to the board, showing that they are about to write down something which is being said. This is unlikely to happen if the pupil is saying something which is irrelevant.
— if the teacher is about to interrupt a pupil's answer it is likely that the pupil is not contributing what the teacher wants to hear.
— a teacher's face often betrays the appropriateness of what the pupil is saying. Frustration, anguish, boredom, are not easily hidden. The look which says, 'Oh, not again Johnny', or 'Well done again, my little pet (aren't I clever to ask you)', can be spotted immediately and recognised by all of the children in a class.

- Is the discussion interesting and meaningful?

As with every other aspect of work in a classroom, there is seldom any point in doing something for its own sake. Children participate enthusiastically if the topic of conversation is about something which interests them. For very young children, the topic needs begin with their own experience. Talk about them, what they do, their homes, their families, their pets, the articles they bring into school etc.

Evaluating discussion

We must now consider what the teacher can do to find out what is happening in the classroom during a discussion, or a period of questioning.

By studying their own techniques in conducting classroom interaction teachers should be able to improve their own practices. To do this, interaction should be recorded. The teacher can ask a colleague to sit in on a session and make notes about what happens. This is not always going to be practical, and in any case requires a collaborator who is familiar with recording techniques, and is known well enough to the children not to influence the proceedings by being there. A far better method is for teachers to tape record the session, and extract the required information for themselves. They will soon be able to see whether questions are open or closed, which pupils have taken significant parts in discussion, and to what extent they dominated the conversation.

A closer analysis is needed to discover from the language the children used the extent to which the conversation developed the children's processes of thinking.

Responses to the evaluation

Teachers can set out a short list of open questions to ensure that they ask a reasonable amount of such questions during a structured discussion. However no one could devise enough questions to cover all the possible ways that a group of imaginative primary school children might develop a conversation.

Some topics of conversation are more suitable to open questioning than others; discussions about poems, emotions, how people ought to behave in particular circumstances etc, are all subjects which offer many open questions.

If the teacher finds that some children do not join in the discussion, they should

consider encouraging group discussion. The groupings must be carefully monitored to ensure that a balanced and sensible discussion is possible in most groups, without the presence of the teacher. The teacher can lead, or simply be a member of, a group of children who are normally reluctant to join in a discussion.

It may be necessary to have one or two groups in the class taking part in a question-and-answer session whilst other children are busy with other activities. Children should be made aware of the importance of discussion as a valuable lead up activity to most group tasks. It will also help them to take everyone's views into account when reaching decisions. Discussion or questioning sessions are not only important in language work. They make a valuable contribution to problem solving in maths, PE and art and craft work, for example.

When a teacher finds that he or she is dominating group conversations, the groups must be left to talk on their own. As it is difficult for a whole class discussion to take place without some intervention by a teacher, group discussion is probably the only way that a dominating teacher can disappear from the limelight. Even then it will take some time for the children to realise that they really can talk without the teacher interrupting.

Activities to encourage talk

To encourage children to join in conversations stimulus activities which will initiate interest and talk amongst the children need to be set up. The activities will depend a great deal on the age of the

children but some of them can be modified to suit any age group. The following examples of suitable activities can be made an integral part of normal classroom work.

- Feely box — a box or bag containing objects which cannot be seen by a child. The child puts his hands into the container and has to guess what the objects are, or describe what they feel like to the other pupils.
- Two children sit on either side of a screen and have identical objects or cards in front of them. One child has to describe an item so that the other can guess which one is being referred to. A variation of this is when one child describes an item, but tries to hide its identity from the other child.

Another alternative is to have grids in front of the children with sets of objects like, for example, those which make up a model farmyard. One child sets up the farm, and then has to describe the plan so that it can be replicated by the child on the other side of the screen.

- With older primary children, *Technical Lego* is a useful vehicle for stimulating talk. If a group of three children are given a box of *Lego*, and set a task, the discussion which follows about how the task might be accomplished is usually quite perceptive. There is a tendency, however, in this kind of situation, for children to use a trial and error approach. After the children have completed their task, they should have the opportunity to see whether it can be done more efficiently.

Although material like *Technical Lego* has explanatory notes showing how to make certain models, these are not helpful if one of the objects of the exercise is to stimulate talk.

- Build a tower — For this exercise the children need old newspapers, and sometimes a pair of scissors. Working in groups they have to construct the tallest possible tower which will stand up on its own.
- Making a game — A small group of children have to make up a game which

can be played in the classroom or playground. When they try to play it, they will probably find that they need to change the rules and this will lead them into detailed discussions.

- Make a shape — During a PE session, ask the children to make individual shapes supporting their weight on, say, two hands and one foot, then two feet and one hand etc. Pairs of children can then join together to make shapes balancing on two hands and one foot etc. Make sure that the children discuss how best this can be done.
- Story-telling — Stories can be used as vehicles for questioning and discussion. They must be used sensitively, however, because the questioning must not interfere with the enjoyment of hearing stories read. A few questions to set the scene are useful, and sometimes questions at the end of the story can clarify certain points and make the story even more enjoyable. In some cases, however, comments or questioning at the end can spoil a good story.

Other ways of stimulating talk include sand and water play, problem solving in maths and re-ordering sentences in a passage of text. Provided the teacher knows why talk is important, and what kind of talk is required, it is easy to create stimulating situations to enable children to discuss, argue, and as a result, think.

Chapter Two

Organisation and management of teaching

Styles

The organisation of a classroom reflects the level of formality which the teacher wants to have in that classroom.

There is much debate in staffrooms and amongst the general public about the level of formality in schools. Schools which are formally run are often seen as 'successful', with their pupils achieving high standards of numeracy and literacy. Informal schools are often regarded as being noisy places, with unruly pupils and scruffy left-wing teachers. These informal schools and the staff are blamed for everything that is wrong in society, from football hooliganism to the economic decline of the country.

Research indicates that a simplisitic sub-division of primary schools or indeed primary classrooms into only two types of teaching does not fully describe what actually happens in primary education.

There is an immense variety and complexity in how individual teachers teach, as indeed there is in how children learn. It may be that a teacher's perceptions of the way children learn dictates to some extent their own style of teaching. Powell (1985), in a study of teaching styles using a System for the Observation of Teaching Strategies (SCOTS), argued that learning is generally carried out in one of four ways:

- by receiving information and explanations from others,
- by interacting with others,
- by thinking through problems,
- by direct experience.

In his study, teachers who regarded the first two as the most important ways of learning, mostly taught on a whole-class basis where learning was convergent. Teachers who stressed the importance of the second two methods took every opportunity to encourage 'open-ended' learning, to develop originality amongst pupils, and to use the pupil's own interests and ideas. They generally used group teaching methods.

Perhaps the most well-known study of teaching styles is the Observation Research and Classroom Evaluation (ORACLE) project (Galton et al 1980). As a result of their observations the researchers divided teachers into six different groups:

- Group instructors

These teachers spent almost 20 per cent of their time working with groups of children, giving them much oral feedback and asking open questions. Their children were able to work alone, and made good progress at some language skills. However, progress at reading and mathematics was limited.

- Class enquirers

This group spent over 30 per cent of the day teaching the class as a whole. They were highly organised teachers, made many statements of ideas, and asked many questions. The children were often 'solitary workers', making little contact with their teachers or other children. Pupils did well at mathematics and in some aspects of language, but made less progress at reading.

- Infrequent changers

This was a highly organised group of teachers who managed to spend 90 per cent of their time with individual children. They made effective changes between class and individual teaching when necessary. Their questioning techniques were good. Their pupils made satisfactory progress in most aspects of the curriculum.

- Individual monitors

These teachers generally taught the children as individuals, but they did not

discuss ideas with them, tending instead to tell children what to do. The children in their classes worked intermittently, and though they made good progress in reading, did less well in other language areas and in maths.

- Habitual changers

This group used class teaching and individual teaching, changing according to the behaviour of the class. They did not ask many open questions, used topic work frequently, and did not spend much time on the basic subjects. Their children made less progress at language work and maths than any of the other groups.

- Rotating changers

Teachers who used this style organised their classes into groups working on different areas of the curriculum. Periodically the groups changed round, which tended to disturb the children. Children in these classrooms did poorly in almost every respect.

The division of teachers into such types has obvious pitfalls and the ORACLE research was conducted some time ago. Probably many primary teachers consider that their teaching style is inadequately represented by these categories. However visitors to primary classrooms will certainly see many teachers working in a similar fashion to those noted in the ORACLE study.

It is interesting in this work to notice the varied use of questioning techniques, and the difference in the teachers' skills in using questioning. There were also important differences in the way teachers managed changes in the way they taught, especially in the change from individual teaching to class teaching. The 'rotating changers' did not manage this effectively, and consequently had discipline problems.

The 'infrequent changers' planned the changes carefully, and perhaps as a consequence, their children made more progress than their counterparts in the other groups.

Interestingly too, the groups showed different patterns of socialisation; the children in the 'class enquirers' group were solitary workers for much of the time. Was it because the teaching was often carried out on a whole class basis?

Where the 'individual monitors' used mainly individual teaching, but used less thought-provoking talk than other teachers, the children were more likely to chat socially during lesson time. Was this a compensation for that lack of incisive talk?

In the ORACLE study the most successful teachers operated in comparatively quiet classrooms, using smooth and efficient organisation techniques which wasted very little time. Clear instructions were given, questions encouraged and answered at length. Children and teachers were in direct contact for a great deal of time and problem-solving activities were used frequently.

What to do about styles

'Every teacher needs a repertoire of teaching styles. At times, for example, every teacher properly adopts the traditional expert authority role providing explanation, information and opinion. At other times teachers need to guide learning less formally, promoting individual and group enquiry, and sharing discovery with the pupils. Teaching styles have to be varied sensitively to match the nature of the work in hand and the characteristics of the pupils, as well as their stage of development.' *(Better Schools* HMSO 1985.)

Of course most teachers use a variety of styles, but often without realising it. There is certainly a need for teachers to consider ways which might improve their practice. One of the first considerations when organising class teaching is to determine what is best taught to the class as a whole, and what is best taught in groups, or on an individual basis. The timing and organisation of changing from one method to another then needs careful manning.

Class teaching

Teaching to the whole class assumes that every pupil can understand what is being taught. Though teachers frequently comment that they have to aim at 'the

T Kerry.

middle', this means that some children are not stretched, whilst others are overtaxed. This creates problems of boredom and disinterest amongst large numbers of pupils. However there are occasions when class teaching is the best method to choose, for example:

- Story time.

This is most obviously a class activity. Disturbance resulting from group work or individual work makes it difficult for a teacher to read a story to one specific group.

- Giving brief class explanations.

New concepts which are being introduced to an individual, or group in the class can be given to the whole class if all the children are going to have to deal with the concepts eventually. However, it is important not to confuse the children who may all be working at different stages of, for example, a maths scheme.

- Demonstrations of the children's work, and sessions where children show what they have brought to school.

These ought to be class activities if the value placed on children's efforts is to be properly emphasised.

- Opening and closing sessions — the times when the teacher says, 'This is what we are going to do today', or, 'Let's get together now for the last ten minutes to see what everyone has been doing'.

These have important implications for control, and for overall organisation.

- Some questioning sessions.

It is more difficult to question a class as a whole as it is clearly more difficult to involve a whole class than a group or an individual. Nevertheless, on some occasions it is necessary to discuss some matters with the whole class. Questioning before or after story time is one such example.

Susan McDonald 1981

Group work

As *Better Schools* (HMSO 1985) points out, we should make a distinction between group activity, when members are co-operating and contributing to a joint activity, and the occasions when, although the children are sitting in groups, they are actually working on their own. In the latter case, the children are grouped together for social reasons. When children are actually working together, the teacher has to decide on whether to group children of similar ability, or whether to have mixed ability groups. Comments on this can be found later in this chapter.

Group work is necessary when the teacher wants the children to participate in a joint activity, for example, problem-solving or, re-ordering a piece of mutilated text as part of a language activity, or carrying out investigations, or making a model. The children also learn social skills during these activities.

Question sessions are more successful with groups than with a whole class. It is easier, for example, to evaluate a session with a few children rather than with many; the involvement of every child in the group can be monitored as the session proceeds.

With proper organisation, children working together in groups can learn actively and co-operatively. Work can be quite accurately matched to the needs of individual children. However, these advantages will not be achieved if the teacher does not understand the purpose of group work, or lacks the organisational skills to make it work effectively. The SCOTS research (Powell 1985) found few teachers who used group methods effectively. Indeed, few class teachers working with groups gained advantages for their children that could not have been gained by perceptive class teaching. Yet the study also found many class teachers who used poor teaching methods, with repetitive work, long queues, and little interaction between themselves and their pupils.

Individual teaching
Individual interaction is continually shown to be important in successful teaching, provided it is used perceptively. In the ORACLE study, individual monitors worked mainly on a one-to-one basis with the children, but in a somewhat perfunctory manner, rather than in a way that enabled children and teachers to develop the children's ideas effectively.

If we accept that every child is at a different stage of development, psychologically, emotionally and physically, it is easy to argue that teaching should predominantly be on a one-to-one basis between teacher and pupil. In practice this utopian view of the teaching process is almost impossible. Many primary teachers have, however managed to work very successfully in this way over the last 20 years. Some would argue that if education is really to be 'child-centred' then teaching ought only to be on an individual basis, particularly with very young children. Unfortunately it is possible that some of the bad press that education has received is a result of teachers trying to teach in this way when, for a variety of reasons they are incapable of doing so. Partly in response to the need for giving more individual attention to pupils, there have been movements over the last ten years to bring parents into classrooms. Some of these initiatives are discussed in other books in this series.

Changing teaching styles

The most common change in teaching methods is from a brief session of class teaching to either group or individual work. At the end of the class teaching sessions, pupils should be told about the changes and how it will affect them. Consider the following points if you want the changes to be effectively carried out.

- The work for each individual or group must be well prepared with all the necessary resources available. If possible, these resources should be split up and placed in various parts of the room so that all the children do not need to go to one place to get paper or scissors etc.

• Explanations for what each group has to do must be brief, with all the children listening to the whole briefing session, before being left to start their work. When a class breaks up to do individual work, it is clearly impossible to brief every child; some children ought to be continuing with activities which they have previously begun. If the teacher wants to change a child's activities, each child can be briefed as the teacher moves around the class. Work cards are often useful in these situations. It is important, though, that the cards are easy to understand.

The change from group or individual work to class teaching usually happens towards the end of a session and gives the teacher an opportunity to display the work of some pupils. At this point a decision has to be made about 'clearing up', and what to do about unfinished work.

If 'clearing up' is to be completed before examples of children's work are to be shown, allow plenty of time for this to be done properly. Demonstrations should not be going on when some children are still at the sink, or picking up scraps of paper. As this is usually difficult to manage it is often best to show work before the final clear up begins.

Unfinished work must either be put away for safe keeping, or given to the children to be completed at home. Such practice may go against the school's policy or the parents' wishes about homework. If the material is kept at school, time must be allowed for it to be finished, even if the teacher has to re-arrange the timetable. Otherwise, the children may feel that some of their work is not highly valued. Many class timetables have a period on Friday afternoon called 'finishing off'. This is not usually the best time for what ought to be one of the most important parts of any piece of work — its completion.

Grouping children

The way teaching is carried out depends on which method the teacher prefers, what is being taught, the resources available, and even the nature of the school building.

In many primary schools, children work in groups for large periods of time during the day. The grouping of the children should be carefully considered.

It is also important to remember that it may be desirable and necessary to change the groups during the course of the day.

Grouping by ability

Putting children of a similar ability together is quite common and often means that the groups remain the same throughout the school year. Sometimes the groups are given 'neutral' names, for example, colours or animals. Giving groups neutral names rather than A, B, C etc, suggests that teachers are not happy with this style of grouping, and are trying to hide the fact that some groups are better than others. Whatever names are used, the children soon learn how these groups are made up. Some parents can become quite worried if their child is in a low ability group.

Several reports have suggested that the brightest children in our primary schools are not being given work to help them reach their full potential. These reports are sometimes used to justify grouping children by ability, and

criticising the use of mixed ability groups. Grouping by ability, however, usually means grouping by ability in mathematics and language work, and these groups remain the same across the whole curriculum. If such grouping really does help children realise their full potential, it presumably only does so in language and mathematics work.

Ability groups are however sometimes the most suitable. The nature of what the children are doing, and the objectives of the activity are important factors to bear in mind.

Ability grouping is preferable for some mathematics work where further progress is entirely dependent on the understanding of previous work. A group of children should not be working together at the same level if they are at different levels of understanding. In these cases it might be better if the children worked individually.

If children are grouped specifically to give them extra help in a particular area of the curriculum, perhaps because they are having difficulties, or because special provision is being given to those who may be classified as 'gifted', it is obviously better to group the children according to their ability.

One of the many criticisms levelled at ability grouping is that the children in the lower ability groups are made to feel inferior. To avoid this teachers can vary the 'end-product' of a piece of work.

Children with lower ability can often speak well and are able to hold their own in a discussion. If the children have to write up discussion a group who are poor at writing may not be able to produce a piece of work to compare with the efforts of other higher ability groups.

Methods of choosing groups of children by ability are often criticised. If teachers rely on their own intuitive knowledge of children, an unconscious bias is likely to appear. Knowledge of the children's parents, home background, accent, dialect, brothers and sisters etc may all influence the teacher's opinions of a child.

If children are tested in order to group them, problems arise when some children gain unexpectedly high or low results, perhaps due to external influences. Choosing the tests is problematic, and if several different tests are used, then there are inevitably difficulties in accumulating the marks. Borderline cases, equal scores, and the limitations on the practical sizes of groups all add to the complications.

When the groups have been set up, a self-fulfilling process begins. Most children only do as well as they and their teacher expect, with the teacher's expectations shown in the levels of the groups.

After a time the groupings may have to be changed. If children in a lower group do well enough to warrant promotion, candidates for demotion have to be found if the groups are to remain in manageable sizes. This leads to competition.

In a classroom where ability groups are maintained throughout the year, competition can be fierce, not only amongst children, but also amongst parents. Parental pressure is often brought to bear on children, school and teachers and this can sometimes affect the social atmosphere of the classroom.

The implications of ability groupings in a mixed age class can give even greater cause for concern. If children of a certain age are put into a lower ability group than younger children it can affect the children's self image and result in behavioural problems.

While many people would apparently disagree with the idea that co-operation is more desirable than competition, the more destructive results of competition amongst young children should not be tolerated, let alone encouraged in school. Since many activities in the primary classroom can be done on a co-operative basis mixed ability groups are certainly to be recommended for some and probably most, of the teaching day.

Mixed ability groups

At a certain time in their primary school life, some children will not want to be grouped with members of the opposite sex. This is not normally taken into account when children are grouped according to their ability, and should not be a significant factor when mixed ability groups are being chosen. More or less equal numbers of girls and boys should be put into each group. The aim is not for the groups to sub-divide into smaller, sex-biased groups, but for the pupils to become less aware of the distinctions between themselves, at least as far as school work is concerned.

The make-up of the groups depends mainly on the pupils themselves, and the teacher's knowledge of them. At the beginning of a new school year, information about the pupils ought to be available from their previous teachers, or if the pupils are new to school, from sources outside the school. When pupils are known to interfere with each other's work, they may need to be kept apart, whereas if two children are firm friends, they may be mutually supportive if they are put into the same group. Sometimes children with similar interests are put together although, in an effort to create groups with a wide range of interests, some teachers deliberately do the opposite.

If there are twins in the class it is probably best to discuss their situation with parents and the children themselves.

Vertical grouping

In many primary schools the number of children entering school each year dictates that there are pupils of different age groups in the same class. For example, if the entry is around 45 children per year, this will almost certainly lead to a mixed age classes. Such classes are 'vertically grouped'.

Some schools deliberately mix age groups even when it is not inevitable. The children usually stay in these classes for more than a year.

The question of whether vertically grouped classes hinder or help the academic progress of children has been the subject of some debate, though it is generally agreed that there are sound social principles behind the ideas. The lack of evidence about academic progress is hardly surprising, since the success or otherwise of any teaching situation depends to a large degree on the class teacher's belief or otherwise in the system being used. There are many variables to be found in a classroom of children of the same age. When these are complicated by introducing different age groups of children, the assessment of progress becomes very complex.

One of the major objectives of vertical grouping is the development of children's social skills. Older children are expected to help in some ways with the education of their young classmates. Indeed the system is sometimes referred to as 'family grouping'.

When the children stay in one class for more than a year, vertical grouping can be a help to the teacher because although some children move on into other classes, some children who are familiar with the routines etc of the class stay on to help the new younger members of the class.

There can be no doubt, however, that in a vertically grouped classroom the teacher's resourcefulness is stretched to the limit, as he or she has to prepare work for the vast range of abilities within the class.

Parental concerns about vertical grouping also have to be answered. Parents need to be informed about the rationale of the system. Teachers in vertically grouped schools also need to ensure that their children have access to those parts of the curriculum which are best taught with children of approximately similar age. Physical education and games lessons, for example, may need two or more classes to be joined together so that the teaching is effective.

Team teaching is one method which allows coherent age groups to be taught together for part of the week, even in a vertically-grouped school.

Class organisation

Team teaching

This system of teaching can only really be used in a suitably designed school. Open plan schools are ideal for this system. In team teaching several teachers join forces and teach their classes together. The children may be taught on a group or an individual basis. An individual teacher may be responsible for teaching a particular aspect of a topic, or one teacher may teach all the pupils, with the other teachers acting in supervisory roles. The resources and facilities of the open areas are available for all of the pupils.

Team teaching enables the special skills of teachers for teaching a specific age group, or for teaching a specific area of the curriculum, to be made available to all the children. It also allows small numbers of children to be taken out of school for visits; this is easier to organise than when a teacher is working alone in a classroom. These visits can be used to enhance the work done in the classroom.

The teaching team is usually lead by one teacher for a specific period of time, or through a particular section of work. The rotation of responsibility is a good opportunity for in-service training, and the system as a whole is full of possibilities for evolving teaching strategies and developing the use of resources.

Mutual trust and a high degree of co-operation between staff is required if team teaching is to be successful. If the teachers do not share a high level of motivation, or have a similar teaching philosophy, then there is little point in attempting to team teach.

Relationships between pupils, and the quality of children's work, may also be influenced by team teaching since children almost inevitably have more freedom than in the usual class-based teaching situation. They can interact with more children, and have to relate to more members of staff. Some children may feel insecure if they are unsure about who is in charge at a particular time. They may even become more difficult to control. It is very important that all the staff involved agree about acceptable levels of behaviour and have the same attitudes towards control.

Because of the different levels of responsibility, teachers need to be aware of what individual children are producing. Definite procedures and patterns of work must be established and agreed by the staff. This makes it easier to keep records about the children's progress.

In planning the curriculum for team teaching, or preparing the timetable for a vertically-grouped class, you may well consider developing an integrated day. However, the use of an integrated day is not limited to classes which are organised in these ways.

The integrated day

This system of organisation involves children in a class working on different curriculum activities at the same time. The children may work in groups, or as individuals; in the latter case, they may change from one activity to another as and when they choose. By the end of the day, children are supposed to have participated in all the activities provided. Some teachers work an integrated day which allows the children to discuss with the teacher their work programme for the day, and then to follow it as individuals, choosing their own order of work.

The integrated day system needs to be carefully monitored to ensure that children follow a coherent pattern of work, and cover the curriculum satisfactorily. The setting up of the classroom each morning, and the recording of what each child has done, are essential if this system is to work effectively. The teacher's work load is immense.

Opponents of this teaching system argue that because of the flexibility and freedom of an integrated day, children who are not highly motivated achieve less in the basic subjects than they do in a more formal teaching system.

If a teacher's records confirm this, it is possible to use a more formal approach for part of the day. For example, certain periods can be used when all the children in the class work on language or mathematics; the remainder of the curriculum can still be taught using an integrated approach. However, if the curriculum is being taught through a thematic approach it is not possible to compromise in this way.

The integrated day gives the children a certain amount of responsibility for their own learning, and as a result they have to use their own initiative. They learn how to gather information and get the habit of perservering in their work. Their learning can be tailored precisely to their own needs.

Organising classroom space

The way a teacher uses classroom space can affect both the way children are organised and teaching strategies. However a room is planned, certain areas are always needed.

Reading areas

Reading areas can be made by arranging and displaying books on suitable shelves. A piece of carpet on the floor, a few chairs and some cushions all help to make the area attractive enough to invite children to read for pleasure. Another similarly inviting area may contain toys or practical apparatus which is used by children everyday. Cupboards and screens can be used to mark out the area.

Art and craft space

An art and craft area should be located

near the sink, if the classroom has one, with at least one large flat area on which children can work. Easels, and a washing line to dry paintings should be included. The materials for art and craft work must be accessible and if a sink is not available, a rota for fetching water needs to be set up.

Storage areas

Two types of storage area are required — one for long-term storage (which can be outside the classroom if space is limited) and one for items in frequent use. There should be rules about access to the storage. Boxes must be clearly marked so that the children and teacher know exactly what is where. Certain children should be responsible for ensuring that the equipment is returned at the end of each day.

Storage space is needed for each child's equipment. If there is no room in the children's tables, blocks of drawers may be used. These must be split up so that the children are not always crowding into one area to find their exercise books or whatever.

Desk arrangements

Enough space should be left in the classroom to group the children's desks as required. The way desks are put together has significant implications for both the children's learning and for their social development. There is some evidence to suggest that when children sit in rows they behave better than when they sit in small groups. Obviously, one reason for this might be that sitting in groups gives children more opportunity to talk to other pupils than when the desks or tables are in rows. For interactive activities, however, rows of desks are clearly inappropriate. Some teachers use a 'horseshoe' arrangement of tables, with one or two clusters of tables outside the 'shoe'. This can be a useful compromise arrangement. If the arrangement of desks is changed at, say, half termly intervals, the children become more aware of their environment and of what goes on in the classroom.

The position of the teacher's desk can change but it is not always necessary for it to be in front of the board. When they are sitting down, the children should be able to see easily both the teacher and the board.

If the teacher's desk faces the main classroom windows, the teacher will not always be able to see clearly the expressions on the pupil's faces. Since children's expressions say a great deal, the teacher should either move the desk, or move around the classroom during the lesson. Walking around the classroom also helps to keep an eye on the children's behaviour and makes the children more attentive to their work.

Any remaining space in the classroom ought to provide flat surfaces, preferably under display boards. These surfaces should be low enough for the children to reach objects laid on them. The display boards should also be low enough for children to see and read their contents.

More ideas about the use and organisation of classroom space can be found in the *Bright Ideas* book from Scholastic.

Chapter Three

The children

Children bring joy to the job of teaching. They bring the freshness and curiosity of youth to the classroom every day.

At 8.45 am every morning a primary teacher welcomes a crowd of excited youngsters, each of whom have something important to tell. Some arrive with a few flowers, others with precious articles which have been brought in especially to show the teacher. All have to be welcomed, listened to, and cared for.

Until they go home at 3.30 pm the teacher is the most important person in their day.

The whole of the education service exists for children — the Department of Education and Science, the LEAs, the university, polytechnic and college departments of education, and the schools. The Ministers of Education, Her Majesty's Inspectors, advisers, officials, lecturers, and teachers, all do their jobs for the benefit of children. However, the only people who really get to know children are the teachers.

Primary classes in the late 1980s usually have at least 30 children. The numbers may vary with the ages of the children and the circumstances of the school, but the official teacher/pupil ratios of around 25 pupils per teacher are not usually a true reflection of actual numbers.

Since each child is an individual, and teachers need to know their charges as individuals, their task is made more difficult by having a large number in the class.

Nevertheless an attempt must be made to get to know the children intimately — their backgrounds, families, interests, strengths, weaknesses, behaviour patterns, learning styles etc.

Record cards

Some of this information is kept on the children's record cards. These records are not standardised throughout the country, and indeed it is only recently that local authorities have begun to standardise record-keeping within their own areas. The wide diversity in the types of records kept, and the differences in attitudes to record-keeping, can cause problems when children move from one school to another, especially if the schools are in different parts of the country.

Information

Usually, records contain two types of information — personal details, and specific curriculum details. In each area of the curriculum there is always a need for detailed records to help in the teaching process. However only a summary of these details is passed on in the child's records at the end of a year. If the records are too detailed a teacher may not have enough time to read them.

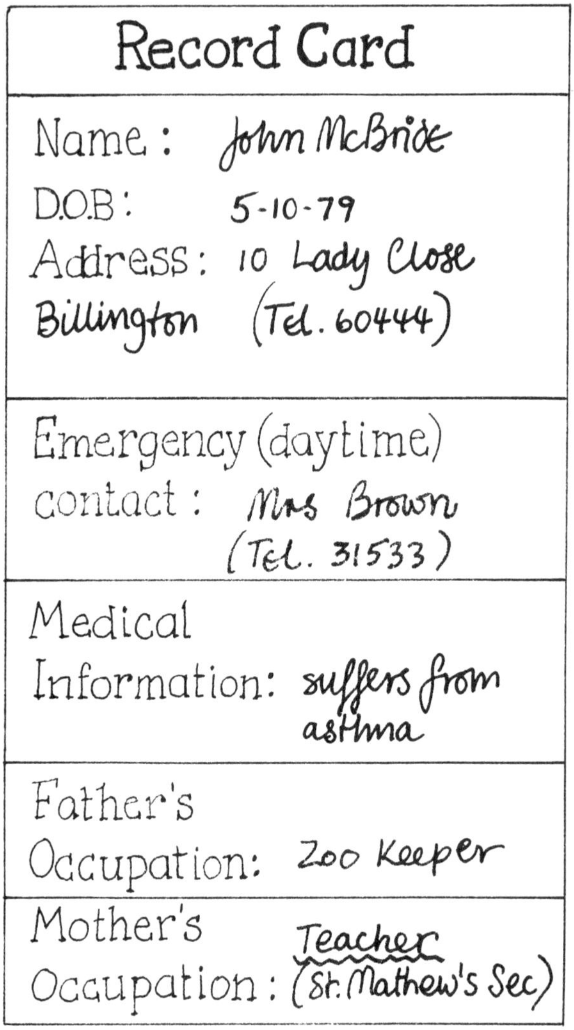 Record Card
Name: John McBride D.O.B: 5-10-79 Address: 10 Lady Close Billington (Tel. 60444)
Emergency (daytime) contact: Mrs Brown (Tel. 31533)
Medical Information: suffers from asthma
Father's Occupation: Zoo Keeper
Mother's Occupation: Teacher (St. Mathew's Sec)

A child's personal details contain information including medical records, with which teachers must become familiar. Confidential notes about children's families are important since children's emotional stability and behaviour are frequently influenced by family life. This kind of information must be accurate, and because it can be sensitive, it is probably better not to keep on written records. The only times when it can be passed on is when another teacher is going to teach the children. Even then, if the information was given in confidence, permission must be given from the source of the information before another teacher is told.

Teachers have to avoid making subjective judgements based on superficial knowledge of children or their records. Children from one parent families do not necessarily have behavioural problems, and children from the inner city areas do not always achieve less than their peers from the more prosperous suburbs.

Knowledge of the children's cultural background is helpful, and children value the teacher's interest in their background and environment. A teacher who has no knowledge of the children's backgrounds and who makes no attempt to find out, undermines the children's confidence in their own identities.

Child development

Records on children help to ensure that they are being taught at an appropriate level.

The notion of child development, which underlies the nature of most teaching in primary schools, influences the nature of these records.

The idea of child development is central to the way that primary teachers see their task. Much of the primary curriculum, including the methods of teaching, has been developed in the light of research which suggests that children go through stages of development. These stages are common to all children, though the rate at which children progress through them varies considerably.

Progress Card Year

Name :
Address :
Age :

Maths

Autumn Term	Spring Term	Summer Term	Remarks

P.T.O.

Every area of children's growth shows a developmental pattern. Here are some brief comments on cognitive development, on one particular aspect of the relationship between cognitive development and language development, and on the development of children's social awareness.

Cognitive development

Teachers must be aware of their pupils' cognitive, or intellectual, development. Research by psychologists such as Piaget, Bruner (1966), Bryant (1974), and Donaldson (1978) has helped teachers to realise the complexity of children's psychological growth, and how it influences their development in schools. This, in turn, has influenced the teachers' work.

It is now generally accepted that children need to build new knowledge, that active involvement is more beneficial to effective learning than the passive 'chalk and talk', method, and that language development is integrally related to intellectual development. Evidence of this can be found in the Nuffield Mathematics Project and in the Schools Council Science Project 5-13 (Ennever and Harlen 1975), both of which are widely used in primary schools. However, teachers often significantly lower the level of practical activity in the classroom as class numbers rise, or as the children reach the top of the primary school. This is usually because the children become more difficult to organise and control.

To ensure that a certain amount of practical activity is carried on higher up the school, a teacher can have limited numbers of groups doing practical work at any time, and rotate the groups. To help out with classroom organisation, it is sometimes possible to ask other adults, such as parents, to come into the classroom on these occasions.

Staged development

The discussion by Piaget and others about staged development is sometimes misinterpreted; the stages are tied to the chronological ages of children, rather than being seen as part of a pattern of continuous growth. This kind of interpretation can lead to children being held back when they may be ready to move on to more complex work. Teachers should not wait passively for evidence that children are ready to move onto the next stage of learning. This often underestimates children's capacities for learning and can result in them being 'understretched'. Learning is a continuous process, and dividing it into stages is simply a convenient way of providing a structure for research work.

I would recommend you to read some of the work of the psychologists mentioned above. In particular, the work of Donaldson is straightforward and of immediate practical value. It includes not only a useful summary of some of Piaget's work, which in its original form is quite difficult to read, but also some important discussions about language development in the classroom.

Language development – reasoning and language

Language development is closely related to intellectual development, and there are many books available on their relationship. *Psychology and Languages* by Clark H and Clark E (1977) is a useful guide. Some ideas about how to improve language development in the classroom can be found in Chapter Two in this book and in more detail in other books in this series.

One aspect of how language interacts with cognitive development needs to be more closely examined. It is the relationship between logical reasoning and language.

We constantly use logic, and the language in which it is expressed, in everyday life. Our normal speech and our teaching practices are full of 'If . . . then' statements and questions which demand inferences.

'If you leave your toys outside, they will go rusty'.

'If you leave out a word, the passage will not make sense'.

'If you do this, what will happen next?'

Inferences

For present purposes, let us consider inferences as being of two types, pragmatic and deductive. Pragmatic inference is when people use existing knowledge and new information to predict possible events. If a teacher talks to children about an experiment they are conducting in science, and asks what they think is likely to happen next, the children are being asked to make pragmatic inferences; they have to give an answer that demands some prediction.

In making deductive inferences, on the other hand, children do not produce anything other than what is already given. The following question, for example, demands deductive inference to answer it correctly.

If Tom is taller than Ben, and Ben is taller than Anna, who is the tallest of the three children?

Here, the answer is locked in the language, for the meaning of the word 'tall' predetermines the answer. Consider also the situation when a child, having read to the teacher a passage about a red bus, is asked about the colour of the bus. A type of referential inference is required. However, if the destination of the bus has not been mentioned, a question on it would make the child use pragmatic inference to find an answer.

In school we are constantly asking children to make inferences, for example, when discussing passages that they have read, when setting comprehension

exercises, when asking questions about the construction of models etc. We use the curriculum to reflect something which is done constantly in everyday life.

It is important for children to learn how to make both pragmatic and deductive inferences, but research reveals that questions which demand pragmatic inference are seldom asked. When they are, teachers often answer the questions themselves.

With suitable practical activities, teachers can help children to speculate about things which can be tested out later on. Appropriate language use is an essential part of this speculation.

Teachers must ensure that their classroom activities, particularly those devoted to encouraging talk (see Chapter 1) allow inferencing skills to be steadily developed throughout the primary years.

The development of social awareness
The level of social awareness of infants new to school depends on many factors — what has happened in their pre-school years, the type of interaction they have had with other adults, the chances they have had to play with other children, and the nature of their home environment, both physical and emotional. Those who have attended pre-school playgroup or nursery, can usually be spotted by the teacher.

Social relationships
It is important that children build up social relationships with other children in school. Obviously there are many differences between children, and it is a mistake to try and make all children participate to the same extent in group activities. Children should begin to see themselves as part of social groups — small friendship groups, the larger class groups, and the group of pupils who attend a particular school. They should become sensitive to the needs and emotions of others in their groups, realise that group membership often entails responsibility, and have confidence to establish their own places within the groups. They should also realise that their contribution and

membership is valued by the other group members.

The process of grouping in schools, discussed earlier, has significant implications for the development of social relationships. One of the main aims of vertical grouping is the social development of children.

The pupils who most need help in social development, and in integrating into the class, are those who are set apart by background or behaviour. For example, if children are not looked after at home, and are consequently dirty and smelly, their classmates will react against them. Parents may tell their children not to sit next to a dirty pupil, perhaps because they are afraid that they might catch head lice.

Children who bully their peers, or aggravate them by poking or pinching, may also be ostracised.

It is difficult for the teacher to avoid a few children becoming segregated and the root causes of the problem have to be tackled. This usually involves the teacher in discussions with parents which though perhaps difficult to arrange, must be attempted. Parents need to be approached carefully in order to avoid embarrassment and animosity. Ultimately, the social services and the educational psychologist may have to be contacted. Meanwhile the teacher ought to do his or her best to ensure that the pupil who is the subject of the discussions is not isolated in the classroom.

Analysing relationships

Generally, children get on well together in a primary classroom but sometimes it is useful for the teacher to look deeper into the relationships. This can be done by using sociometric analysis, an unfashionable technique, but one which still gives valuable information to teachers. In its simplest form, children are asked to write down in confidence the names of children they consider to be their best friends, or the children they would most like to sit next to in class. The teacher then makes a plan of where the children sit with arrows illustrating the children's responses. By varying the questions, the analysis can be made more complex, and will show the teacher which children are, in fact, isolated. This kind of analysis often reveals important features of classroom social interactions which are hidden by in the normal hurly-burly of classroom life. Note, however, that under no circumstances should the results of this kind of analysis be shown to the children.

As with most aspects of learning, children's social development improves through active involvement in that learning. Why not try some of the activities listed here:

- Many books relate stories of children who have no friends, who are ignored or bullied by their peers. You can use these stories as the basis for discussion, drama and role play to bring out their social relevance.

- Children can make up games. When the games are played the rules usually have to be modified, thus bringing the children's attention to the need for co-operation and 'fair play'.
- When choosing teams for games, the 'selector' should be changed on each occasion. The teams should have equal ability as far as possible. Juniors can discuss why this is desirable.
- In recent years there have been increasing demands on schools to collect for various charities. Giving to those in need, and the responsibilities of those who are financially well off towards those who are less well off, are obvious topics for discussion and debate in a classroom. With older children the debate can be extended to include decision making, for example, about the distribution of goods at the end of harvest festival. In this way, the children are involved in deciding who is to benefit from their generosity, as well as simply organising the collections.
- Children can help each other by using 'peer group' tutoring in reading. This increases their level of social development, as well as increasing the levels of reading skills in their classes. This activity is best used in vertically-grouped classes.

In practice, the procedure is rather like 'paired reading' which involves parents. The children work in pairs, one of whom has a reading age at least two years different from the other. The teacher must choose the pairs carefully to ensure that they will really work together. When

the session begins, the children read aloud together. The child with the lower reading age indicates with a tap on the desk when he or she wants to continue reading alone. The progress of the children should be carefully monitored. Short, frequent sessions are preferable.

Obviously, there can be difficulties. The teacher must outline exactly what has to be done to make the sessions effective, but must guard against giving one group of children a feeling of superiority or privilege. Parents need to be informed about the scheme, and if they object to having their child tutored by other children, should be able to withdraw them from the scheme. Some advocates of the scheme suggest that the tutors keep records about their partners. For obvious reasons this should be treated with extreme care, with only simple details of the reading sessions being recorded.

Children with particular needs

While teachers try to give equal attention to all the children in their classes, it is inevitable that some children will take more of their attention than others. This may be a deliberate policy if the teacher feels that some children need more attention than others. Sometimes it is due to pressure from headteachers, or other interested parties who feel that certain children warrant extra attention.

Children with special needs

Since the Warnock Report and the 1981 Education Act a large number of children from special schools have been integrated into ordinary primary schools. The report suggests that one in 20

children could at some stage in their school lives be considered to have special needs.

Although all children have the right to be taught the same curriculum, teachers obviously have to organise their work so that children with special needs gain the maximum benefit from that curriculum. For this to be effective, careful planning is required.

It is important to determine which skills and concepts are to be covered in specific lessons. The teacher also has to decide which teaching method is best for achieving the aims of the lessons. Individual teaching may often be the most appropriate way to teach a particular item, but if you decide on group work, the make-up of the groups needs to be considered. In essence, the principles of special needs teaching are no different from those of good primary practice, with extra attention being given to some of the children.

Ideas to consider

- Try to base tasks on the children's own experience. Use what children already know, and are able to do, as a starting point for further work.
- Break the tasks down into small units, with definite, but small progressive steps.
- Use a good deal of repetition and reinforcement.
- Have as many practical resources available as possible, and ensure that they relate to the tasks in hand.

Above all, remember that the main cause of difficulty for primary children with special needs is their lack of success. The teacher must ensure that the children experience success as often as possible, that they are given constant encouragement and that the children's efforts are sincerely praised.

Gifted children

Everyone should reach their full potential and the primary school has a significant part to play in helping pupils to realise theirs. However, evidence suggests that those who are the most capable, are the least likely to achieve that goal. One reason is that hard-pressed teachers often expect bright children to do well with a minimum amount of attention from them.

The belief that some of our most gifted pupils are being held back in primary schools has lead to various initiatives being developed to try to give them special help. One of these is to regularly remove the children from their classes. They are then given specially prepared high level work in certain curriculum areas. Some local authorities have established weekend or half-term courses for gifted children. Identifying gifted children does have its difficulties. It has been suggested that anyone with an IQ of over 140 is gifted, but this is unfair to those children who are perhaps gifted in music or sport, art or craft. In fact, the term gifted, when it is applied in a school, usually refers to those who are very competent in academic subjects. Those who are capable in other areas do sometimes receive extra help, in school clubs for example, but it is often left to enthusiastic parents to arrange coaching etc. Since this usually costs extra money, poorer parents are often unable to meet the costs and their children's gifts are simply not developed.

It is possible, however, to develop the potential of gifted children in the ordinary classroom. The following are important points for all teachers to consider:

- Make sure that the work which is prepared for all pupils is stretching them to the limits of their ability.
- Ideas and resources should be available for pupils who finish work quickly. Provided that their work has reached a satisfactory standard, let them develop their ideas, rather than simply repeat work. For example, on one occasion when a group of children were working with prime numbers, one of the children recalled seeing an article in a newspaper on the subject. The article was found, and followed up by some children who were very good at maths — a much more interesting way of

developing the theory of prime numbers than sticking to the maths scheme being used.

- Try to ensure that children who are gifted in any particular field have the opportunity to reach their full potential in that field, so regarding all talents as being equally important.
- Obtain advice and expertise from specialists in the school, and don't forget that staff, and sometimes children, will have hobbies and interests which make them 'experts' within the school.

Chapter Four

The curriculum

The curriculum is not just what is taught by a teacher. It consists of many activities which together are aimed at helping children reach educational aims. Objectives have to be set, content determined, teaching organised, and the whole process evaluated.

In some schools each of these facets of the curriculum is constantly reviewed, and even those teachers who argue that there have been few changes in their own schools will at least have been involved in some of the debates which have raged around curriculum issues.

- Should schools concentrate more on their academic rather than their social roles?
- What influence should schemes of work have on the curriculum?
- What is the place of religious education in the curriculum?
- How can the curriculum take account of the technological revolution which is changing so much in our society?
- How can the curriculum cope with the developing role of parents in education?
- How can a curriculum be developed which is relevant in a multicultural society?
- What are the implications for the curriculum of the integration of children with special needs into primary schools?
- What impact will the Education Reform Bill have on the curriculum?

These are a few of the countless important issues which have to be discussed when debating the primary school curriculum.

Educational reform

At the end of 1987 the government introduced to Parliament a bill containing many proposals for educational reform. The Great Education Reform Bill, as it has come to be known, is due to receive Royal Assent in the early autumn of 1988. It has three sections; Part 1 about schools, Part 2 about Higher and Further Education, and Part 3 about education in Inner London.

Part 1 includes several proposals which have important implications for primary schools. These deal with open enrolment for schools, the delegation of responsibility for school budgets, the possibility of schools 'opting out' of the state sector to become grant maintained schools, and the introduction of a national curriculum.

Provision for more open enrolment to schools is intended to give parents greater opportunity to send their children to schools of their choice, thus increasing the rolls of the more popular schools and forcing the less popular schools to improve their 'marketability'. Critics of this idea suggest that it only increases the choice for those parents who are able to transport their children easily, and that it will create 'sink' schools in poor areas.

The proposal that schools ought to have control of their own budgets, reflects the apparent success of pilot schemes in various parts of the country. There has been criticism that headteachers and governors, who will become largely responsible for the allocation of money for salaries, books and equipment, heating, lighting, cleaning etc, many not have sufficient expertise to spend the money wisely.

The provision for 'opting out' enables the governors of a school to apply for grant maintained status. They may initiate a ballot of parents, and in the event of a successful result, make formal application to the Secretary of State.

The abolition of ILEA (part 3), has been hotly disputed. One of the major concerns in the latter case is that the education of, for example, children from minority groups, and children with special needs, will receive less attention than was the case in ILEA.

The section which advocates a national curriculum, is the one which has received most attention.

A national curriculum

The bill notes that a national curriculum ought to include the 'core' subjects of English, mathematics and science. These are to take up the majority of time in primary schools. However, technology, history, geography, art, music and PE are seen as important 'foundation' subjects which children need to study. Attainment targets are to be set, and children to be tested at four 'key' ages: seven, 11, 14 and 16.

In many ways a national curriculum is to be recommended. Indeed, most children have been taught a broadly agreed national curriculum for a number of years. Nevertheless, the government plans have aroused opposition about the number of the foundation subjects, about the introduction of 'bench marks' or levels of attainment, and about the notion of 'testing' in general.

The idea of 'bench marks' is attractive to some because it is seen as a means of testing the efficiency of the education system and of comparing the schools in it. Those who oppose the establishment of bench marks think that their use threatens the quality of the teaching process, and may override the concern which teachers legitimately have for the needs of individual children. There is disagreement between those who suggest that learning the content of the curriculum is an end in itself, and those who see the learning of content as a means of achieving higher level goals. Without doubt there can be disadvantages in testing children at specific times during their school career, especially in the primary stage.

Testing can easily concentrate on trivialities, the regurgitation of learning facts, rather than the ability to think through problems.

Tests can dictate what is taught in the classroom, with teachers teaching to the tests, or even teaching children some of the tricks which may help in taking tests.

The actual process of testing is almost certain to lead to a number of children seeing themselves as failures, since only a limited number of children can pass tests. When the tests are set some children will sit down to take them knowing that whilst others are busily engaged in succeeding, they can scarcely understand the questions. Frustration, rage, anger, and humiliation may result from this.

A group, led by Professor Paul Black, was set up by the Secretary of State to make recommendations about the assessment of children's performance, and progress across the subjects in the National Curriculum. This task group (TGAT), reported in January of 1988.

They recommend that the core and foundation subjects be divided into components, for example, listening, speaking, reading and writing for languages. The components are then to be divided into ten performance levels, covering the age ranges seven to 16. Children will be assessed on each of the components at these levels. It is further recommended that formal and informal methods of assessment ought to be used, and that the results ought to be moderated at meetings of teachers. This moderation process can give rise to feedback on the curriculum. The formal part of the assessment, TGAT suggested, should be closely allied to tasks which pupils are used to doing, and be tied to national objectives. Each pupil will have a profile of attainments built up over their school life.

The recommendations of the TGAT report clearly make an attempt to overcome some of the problems already noted above, but before they can be put into operation there is an enormous amount of work to be done in every subject — to set the components and the levels, to set some standards for the teacher assessed part of the testing, and to determine the tasks to be completed by the children.

While the national curriculum will have considerable impact on schools in the future, there are curriculum issues which teachers have been concerned about for some time, and which are having an immediate influence upon schools. While we mentioned several of them earlier in this chapter, let us now look more closely at four of them.

The curriculum in a pluralistic society

Britain in the 1980s is a society of many people from different races, who have a wide variety of cultural backgrounds, and an equally wide variety of aspirations for themselves and their children. This society is reflected in the school population; the number of people from the non-indigenous population is much higher in some areas than in others, so schools in certain areas of the country have a higher proportion of children from ethnic minority groups than others.

Cultural groups

Ethnic minority groups tend to live in decaying urban areas, with poor housing and facilities. A good deal of evidence suggest that these groups suffer particularly from unemployment, and that the chances, for example, of a young black leaving school without qualifications are high.

The deprivation of some groups in our society contributes to tensions in local communities; in some instances this leads to disturbances and occasionally riots in the cities. Inevitably the tensions are reflected in schools. Schools should be starting points for improving relationships between different cultural groups. Until recently the emphasis on cultural differences in Britain was on assimilation or absorption of ethnic minority groups into British society. Now, however, there is greater acceptance of cultural pluralism and the belief that various cultural groups can add to and enrich society as a whole. The importance of retaining cultural identity is now widely recognised. Aspects of different cultures such as languages, should be nurtured for the benefit of society as a whole. By valuing a culture, this helps to preserve and develop the feelings of pride and identity which are so important to an individual pupil's self-concept. This ideal of cultural pluralism must be nurtured by schools.

Social awareness

Schoolteachers throughout the country need to ensure that their curriculum takes account of our diverse society. Just because your school, or local authority, has no children from minority groups, there is no reason to exclude work about these groups from your curriculum. On the contrary, it is more important to teach children about minority groups if they are unlikely to meet children from different cultural backgrounds during their school days. Otherwise, when they leave school, they may take with them some of the prejudice and ignorance which has caused so much damage to race relations in the past.

It has been suggested (see Houlton 1986) for example, that schools' responses to the challenge of cultural diversity among their pupils can be grouped under four headings:

- Treat them all the same.
- Refer to them as having Special Needs.
- Use a compensatory model.
- Develop a curriculum with multicultural aspects. None of these responses has proved to be satisfactory.

Houlton goes on to point out that a curriculum which merely makes use of interesting items from different cultures is likely to be inadequate unless it also attempts to counter the basic inequalities in our society. In other words, schools must have an anti-racist policy.

Religious education and assemblies

Religious education

In state schools, there has to be a regular school assembly, and provision for teaching RE. In teaching RE, staff are not supposed to indoctrinate their pupils. Teachers may, however, withdraw from teaching RE and similarly parents can ask for their children to be withdrawn from RE lessons and assemblies.

Since many religions have played a significant part in world history, it seems logical that pupils should learn about the continuing importance of religions. Although most primary teachers have taught RE in schools for many years, they have mostly dealt with Christianity. Many different religions are now represented by the pupils in our schools and these religions must be reflected in RE teaching today.

As with every other area of the curriculum, religious education must involve learning processes as well as teaching information. Accordingly, children should consider the issues involved in religious belief, and be encouraged to reach some conclusions for themselves. Teachers who have strong religious faith may believe that it is part of their calling to convert others to that faith. Young children are particularly susceptible to such evangelism and it has no place in our schools.

One of the best ways of introducing young children to religion is through the stories which are part of most world religions. By using stories from different religions we are also introducing multicultural aspects into the curriculum.

Assemblies

In many schools, teachers are expected to take turns in leading assemblies. Some find this irksome, but the alternative of having the same one or two teachers (usually head or deputy) take assembly, often results in a repetitive, unimaginative start to the day. When taking assembly, it is important to try and meet certain criteria:

- If possible, there should be some continuity between assemblies, just as between a series of lessons.
- An assembly can provide a possible starting point for other teaching during the day. If so, it is useful if the teacher taking assembly circulates notes to other staff, preferably a few days in advance.
- An assembly must have an objective; often making a moral point.
- An assembly must catch the children's interest. Using familiar themes is a good way of doing this.

Here are two examples. The first assembly was initiated by the need to encourage children to share and not to be greedy.

This was the plan:

- The children were questioned about food — favourite foods, foods from other lands, types of food, and the sensation of feeling hungry.
- Items of food — an apple, a tin of beans, a box of cornflakes, were hidden in turn under a cloth. The children had to ask questions to find out what foods were being hidden.
- The children were shown anagrams of the names of foods and children were asked to solve them.
- When the children's interest had been thoroughly aroused, a short discussion introduced the idea of greed, and the children were asked to think of stories about 'greediness'.
- The story of 'Mr Greedy' was read, and the moral drawn.

The second assembly was about Christmas customs.

The assembly went as follows:

- The giant school letter box was set up in the hall before the children entered. A small child was hiding inside the box.

• A child was invited to post some cards.
• The teacher posted more cards, which were promptly pushed out of the box. The teacher tried again to post the letters, with even less success. A groaning sound was heard from behind the box! The teacher asked the children what the problem could be and the envelopes were examined. They did not have enough information on them to reach their destination.
• The need for giving full information on envelopes was emphasised.
• The child behind the post box came forward, and the children were warned strongly about not hiding in boxes etc.
• A discussion on Christmas cards followed which eventually lead to further assemblies on Christmas customs.

Class assemblies are important features of many primary schools. They give children an opportunity to 'perform', sometimes in front of parents as well as the school.

Points to remember
All the children in the class must have the opportunity to take part. Children who are most capable and/or extroverted must not always have the main parts. Children who have learning difficulties, or who are shy, can gain confidence by taking part in the class assemblies.
• Children who, for whatever reason, do not want to take part, should be gently

but firmly encouraged. They should not be forced to participate, though. A lack of confidence can sometimes be overcome by using groups of children, for example, singing, dancing, and marching.

- Singing, dancing, marching and mime add excitement to an assembly. No one who has seen a whole school lead 'pied-piper' style out of the assembly hall and around the school building during a class assembly will forget the experience.
- A class assembly must be simple and straightforward to organise, allowing children who have been absent to join in at short notice.
- Dressing-up is a great attraction for the children who are taking part, and it catches the audience's attention very quickly. This is an important factor, particularly if the audience is made up of very young children.
- Learning lines should be avoided if possible. Words which are virtually spontaneous are more likely to be remembered by the participants.
- Assemblies which are produced co-operatively by more than one class can set the scene for more co-operative teaching, and help to eliminate the element of competition which occurs in some schools.

Used perceptively, class assemblies can be extremely worthwhile, but if they become competitive, with classes and teachers trying to outdo each other, their value is lost. Teachers involved in class assemblies must ensure that their preparation does not take too much time.

Schemes of work

It is odd that when evidence suggests that expenditure in schools on books, paper, pencils etc is falling in real terms, there is a boom in the sales of commercially-produced work schemes, particularly for mathematics and language. In some local authorities, not only is there pressure on teachers from publishing houses to buy their schemes but also from local advisers.

Schemes of work have, for a long time, been a vital part of the curriculum in many primary schools.

They have many advantages. Teachers of children of the same year groups can ensure that they are teaching their pupils roughly the same things. They also allow teachers of one year groups to have a good idea of what is being learned by the children in other year groups.

Not all schemes of work are commercially produced. Some are written by teachers within a school, some by teachers from a group of primary schools which serve a local secondary school. Such schemes can be written with particular children in mind, and are tailored to meet their precise needs. The schemes are kept up-to-date by a continuous process of curriculum development which reflects the changing environment of the school, the changing needs of the children and the strengths and interests of the staff. Involving teachers in such curriculum development means that they have a continuing commitment to the schemes.

Commercial schemes

The commercially-produced schemes, which until recently were used in most primary schools alongside those written by teachers, were mainly 'core' schemes. They provided a comparatively small-scale teaching resource. For example, a reading scheme would contain a set of graded reading books and perhaps some

comprehension cards, but little other material. A mathematics scheme would contain a teacher's book, a set of graded books for the children, and perhaps some extension exercises on sheets which could be duplicated if required. A good teacher went beyond the books, tapping his or her own resourcefulness and expertise, and that of other teachers. No-one expected the scheme to be a complete course.

Development

Over the last few years, however, all-embracing schemes have been developed, particularly in language and maths. These profess to cover every aspect of the subject, and suggest implicitly that all the children should cover all these aspects. The schemes are very expensive, often costing well over £1,000.

As the concept of the core scheme is being considerably extended, in many instances the teacher-produced schemes, with their various benefits, are being stifled.

Problems

In schools which adopt all pervasive maths and language schemes, teachers can become over-reliant on them, and fail to introduce aspects into the lessons which reflect their own expertise and enthusiasm. Teachers become more concerned with getting through the books than with using practical activities to develop children's learning. They also feel that they can't justify enough time to exploit children's enthusiasm for aspects which come outside the scheme.

Economic considerations, too, have played a part in the subtle shift in the role of schemes from servants to masters. When a school spends a large amount of money on a scheme, teachers feel obliged to use all the material.

Some schemes have not been thoroughly evaluated, either in terms of genuine academic research, or on an *ad hoc* basis by individual schools or local authorities.

Which head, having spent most of the school's annual budget on a scheme, is going to produce information which discounts its value? Which teacher, perhaps new to a school, is going to speak out against such a costly resource, especially if others on the staff seem to use it whole-heartedly? Which publisher is going to fund research which may cast doubts on the wisdom of the schools buying their products?

The all-encompassing maths schemes were produced before similar language schemes. Many primary teachers feel that maths is their weakest subject. Some years ago as criticism of maths teaching in primary schools grew, the increase of use of support material such as schemes of work became more justifiable. As teachers became more familiar with large scale maths schemes and relied on them more and more it was only a small step to a similar expansion in the core language schemes.

While some teachers may need a lot of assistance in mathematics, few need similar help in language. Though the value of schemes as contributory resources cannot be doubted, the use of the large schemes available implies that a few writers are able to develop a complete curriculum, suitable for every child.

A curriculum for the future

In some respects, today's society is changing faster than at any time in history. Schools have to teach children to adapt to cope with massive changes in their life styles, to handle a vast increase in the amount of knowledge available, and to satisfy society's need for greater awareness of science and technology.

Leisure time

There is already a need to prepare today's pupils for their increased leisure time. This is not only because the level of unemployment is likely to remain high, but because for those in work, the number of holidays is increasing, as the

length of the working day decreases. The implications for the primary curriculum are that children should be encouraged to join in a whole range of leisure time activities, and learn how to get enjoyment and satisfaction from them.

Study skills

As the amount of available knowledge increases citizens of the future will have to know how to access information. The ability to remember a large amount of facts may still be helpful, but it is going to be much less important than it used to be.

Basic study skills, such as the use of a book's contents page and indexes, skimming and scanning skills in reading, note taking and summarising in writing etc, are often neglected in primary schools and this trend will have to be reversed.

Science and technology

Our future society will need more people with a scientific and technological background. Yet there is evidence that science is neglected in primary schools. Whilst they are regarded as being important, physical sciences usually take second place to biological sciences, with little practical work being done.

At the primary stage, the content of scientific work is not as important as teaching children the scientific method. Observing and verifying allow children to make accurate predictions, and to gain a practical understanding of the world in which they live. Their curiosity can be harnessed by good science teaching at the primary level.

The primary curriculum must also teach children to use the electronic tools of the present and the future, by giving them access to modern technology. Society's use of computers, word processors, videos etc is now enormous and the primary curriculum ought to allow all children to use these resources as general teaching aids.

While the primary curriculum often seems to focus on relatively small concerns the larger issues described above have to be emphasised if primary schools are really going to serve the needs of children in the future.

Chapter Five

The school

Although all primary schools have some common features, each has its own ethos, partly created by the building itself, the local environment, but also due to the different methods of organisation and the different ways that schools approach the curriculum. Even in the same authority, sometimes in the same street, two primary schools may operate in entirely different ways.

Philosophy and prospectus

It was partly the diversity amongst schools which caused the Secretary of State for Education in 1987 to call for a national curriculum.

Those who are against a national curriculum believe that it will bring about dictatorial teaching methods and will consequently limit the authority of heads, as well as the choice parents have in selecting a school for their children.

The diversity of the present system means that most teachers agree with their own school's philosophy. They can use teaching methods which they believe work. These are important factors in maintaining the morale and commitment of the teaching force.

Information about the school's approach to the curriculum, discipline, uniform standards, out-of-school activities etc have to be available in a school prospectus, which gives parents some idea of the general ethos of the school. It should also help teachers who are considering applying to the school for a post.

In extreme cases, where

communication between staff and head is limited, the prospectus may help current staff to understand the kinds of approaches to education their headteacher wishes to encourage!

Allocating responsibility

The main feature which influences how primary schools are run is the method of organisation and management of the school.

Until 1987, the structure of management in schools was a hierarchy of the head, deputy and scale post holders. Although the new contractual arrangements are changing this organisation, it seems likely that for the next few years the old system will continue to influence the allocation of duties in schools. However, the new method of payments in primary schools does not allow as many extra payments as was possible before 1987.

Primary schools have always differed in the allocation of responsibilities, though post holders were usually responsible for curriculum areas, and higher paid staff responsible for management and policy. This is not likely to change much in the near future.

Sharing expertise

However, although responsibility has been assigned in this way for years, the HMI report of 1978 noted that an individual teacher's expertise was often not shared with other staff members. Schools should be organised so that teachers' expertise can be shared on in-service training days, and by teachers teaching together. The Grant Related In-Service Training scheme (GRIST), which came into operation in 1987, is helping this type of sharing to take place.

Structuring responsibility

The role of teachers who have curriculum responsibility is largely determined by particular circumstances. Job descriptions are sometimes written, which follow the suggestions of the Cockcroft Report (HMSO 1982), that a co-ordinator (in this case for maths) should prepare schemes of work, provide guidance and support for other staff, monitor progress, diagnose areas where extra support is needed, and initiate in-service training.

Such a structured approach based on curriculum leadership did seem to work, for when post holders were able to plan and supervise programmes of work, standards appear to have been raised (HMSO 1978).

The most common criticisms of primary school management is that although heads and deputies have usually attended management courses, they often have limited experience of putting theory into practice before reaching senior positions. In large primary schools, responsibility can be given for organising the upper, middle and lower parts of the school, or even year groups within one of these broad sections. Such experience is vital for aspiring heads and deputies.

Training

Training opportunities for roles with extra responsibilities must always be taken. GRIST schemes should lead to the development of courses specifically for curriculum leaders. For those new to the profession, it is worth noting that the

government is concerned that all primary teachers should be equipped to take particular responsibility for one aspect of the curriculum, and to act as consultants to other staff (HMSO 1983). Teacher training courses are already taking this into account; it will obviously be a feature of the primary teacher's role in future.

Staff relationships

Relationships between staff play a large part in how the school functions. Particularly in small schools, any animosity or mistrust between staff can interfere with the children's education.

Close friendships are not common to every school staffroom; the range of interests, ages and experience of the teachers is too great. Nevertheless, teachers should respect each other's professionalism. However, this can be difficult during periods of industrial action.

The industrial action which preceded the imposed contract of 1987, brought about a slump in morale throughout the teaching profession. This was partly caused by friction amongst colleagues who had previously been working closely together.

Such friction is bound to affect teaching in schools. Team teaching, for example, and indeed any real initiative in curriculum development, needs a high degree of trust and understanding for it to be successful; just as everyone's strengths are utilised and demonstrated, so everyone's weaknesses also become apparent. A lot of mutual trust is required before teachers will allow their weaknesses to be revealed.

The head and deputy headteacher
The head and deputy have a crucial role to play in forming good staff relationships. Traditionally, the deputy has been a link or mediator between head and staff, though it is not clear why this should be so. Indeed, job descriptions for deputy heads seldom mention this explicitly.

In some schools, the headteacher is regarded with more mystique than in others. In small schools, where the head is a part-time or full-time teacher, the barriers which often exist between the head and other staff break down. In large schools, heads must be sure that they are regarded as members of staff, and not as distant, perhaps authoritarian, figures.

In terms of experience which they will have gained over a number of years in the classroom, headteachers should be seen by other staff members as useful resources. They should be able to give advice, for example, in dealing with outside agencies, or in enlisting the help of support services. While perceptive heads anticipate where and when their help is likely to be needed, they cannot always predict when their advice is required. Class teachers and headteachers must, therefore, communicate regularly with each other in informal, casual conversation as well as in private formal interviews.

A headteacher's involvement in appraisal may have an adverse effect on the development of satisfactory relationships between him or herself and other staff. In this case, the liaison aspect of the deputy head's role may have to be more clearly defined.

Staff meetings

Most schools hold formal staff meetings. In some primary schools, particularly where there are very few staff, staff meetings are rare events. In small schools it is easier for information to be passed to teachers informally. However, in large schools some members of staff can easily miss opportunities to discuss important issues if an informal system is the only one in use.

Some schools have staff meetings as often as once a week; others, as infrequently as once a term. The contractual arrangements of 1987 have enabled staff meetings to be held regularly.

Staff meetings are probably the most appropriate times for staff to participate in decision-making in schools. Unless the number of staff is so large that general discussion is quite impossible, everyone including ancillary staff should be invited to the meetings. Controversial issues must be discussed whenever necessary, and an agenda must be properly set out so that every member of staff can bring up points of concern.

In a few schools, members of staff are given the chance to lead staff meetings.

This practice gives teachers useful experience and may even help staff meetings to run more smoothly.

Where staff meetings are properly led, and used constructively, teachers are likely to attend willingly, and with some degree of enthusiasm.

Relationships between staff, and the attitude of senior staff to involving everyone at a staff meeting, are major factors in determining the effectiveness of staff meetings. All participants should be able to recognise clearly their organisation, content and purpose.

Relationships with the community

A school's philosophy of education reflects the views of the teachers, parents, LEA and governors. A primary school is not a self-contained unit, but an integral part of the community. Local authorities, like Coventry, have made significant progress in recent years in developing the idea of community education.

Organisations in that city such as the CDA (Community Development Association) continue to make education an issue within the local community.

The notion of a community school has a wide variety of interpretations. For some schools the more immediate concern is to involve parents in the school.

The school and the parents

While the idea of having parents in school is not new, it has only recently gained significant publicity. The educational and social value of involving parents in school is unquestionable. For further information on parental involvement, see *Parents in Schools* in this series.

We will look more closely here at the practical considerations of involving parents in the school for educational purposes.

Getting started

Firstly, teachers wanting to work with parents in the classroom, must have the permission of the head, and would be well advised to have the support of other staff. It is difficult, and often embarrassing, to ask parents to work in a classroom, but be unable to invite them into the staffroom for coffee because of the resentment of other teachers. Some schools convert a spare room into a parents' room, but while it is a good idea to have a parents' work room, the staffroom is the best place to relax in.

One of the main objections to having parents in school is that conversations about children may be overheard by parents and retold outside the school. Also, off-the-cuff remarks which may insult children may be taken by parents as an indication of a teacher's poor attitude towards particular children, or towards children in general. The only way to overcome these problems is for a responsible member of staff to speak to parents about the need for confidentiality, and for teachers who regularly use insulting language about children in the staffroom, to recognise the shortcomings of such a practice, even when parents are not present.

When the head has given permission and the staff are generally in favour, the teacher needs to explain to the parents why they have been invited to school. It is probably best to have parents start in one class, or in one area of the school, eg the nursery. After parents have been informally briefed, a letter is usually the best way of attracting parents to an informal meeting to discuss the project.

Choice of parents

Problems can arise if some parents are invited into the classroom while others are excluded. Some teachers choose between those parents who they think will make the most valuable contributions, and those who they think will be of little help in the classroom. Though this may seem to make sense, these choices are usually based on the teacher's biased view of the parents.

All parents have to be given the opportunity to participate in some aspect of classroom work, and if a large number want to help out, a rota must be used.

Organisation

How parental involvement is organised depends on what type of involvement is required, and the age group of the children. An informally organised nursery allows more parents to be in the classroom at a particular time than is usually possible in a junior class. Whatever the age groups, however, the following points should be considered.

- It is not usually a good idea to let parents work with their own children on an individual basis, unless the teacher wants the parents to try out some activities which might be followed up at home.
- A system ought to be worked out so that parents come into the classroom on a regular basis. The classroom must be prepared for the parents' visits and parents need to realise that if they do not turn up or are late, they can disrupt the organisation and efficient working of the classroom. Obviously, some difficulties may arise but it is important to try to make the system run as smoothly as possible.
- Parents who help out at school and have other pre-school age children should be encouraged to bring their younger children to school if at all possible. A complete family in school will often encourage everyone concerned to see the real advantages of encouraging home/school contact.

There are many ways that parents can help in the classroom. At the most basic level they are extra adults who can relate to the children. Ancillary staff can also fulfil this role, and the teacher needs to form good relationships with them just as with parents.

Ancillary helpers

This group of people includes the school secretary, the caretaker, the cleaners, classroom helpers etc. They have always played a most important role in the effective running of schools, and have been regarded by most teachers as essential helpers. Unfortunately due to recent cut-backs, some local authorities have made many ancillary staff redundant, or have significantly altered their jobs; the hours school secretaries work have been cut, and ancillary assistants in junior schools have lost their jobs.

In reception and infant classrooms, however, ancillary helpers are still employed. Often, they have a long experience of the school and neighbourhood, and they have learned to work with many different teachers. They know the children, and their families, and the school procedures.

Ancillary workers should be valued in school, and they should be encouraged to participate in all aspects of classroom management and in the curriculum.

Caretakers, too, frequently have long experience of the school and of the local community. Their attitude to their work has a significant impact upon the school.

Teachers can do much to help caretakers and cleaners in their work by keeping their rooms reasonably tidy. In any case this helps to keep equipment intact and in working order. Learning to keep their room tidy is also an important element of school life for children. Clearing up should be organised effectively, and become a feature of classroom routine.

Buildings

The design of a school influences what goes on in it but often it can't easily be altered to reflect the school's philosophy. The type of building usually depends on the age of the school; some teachers are still teaching in schools over 100 years old. In these schools the windows are high and narrow, toilets may be in the playground, and playing space limited.

More recently, schools have been built on a quadrangle design with classrooms grouped around an area of grass or garden. Outside corridors usually link the classrooms. In the 1960s and 1970s, open-plan schools were built with large windows, and open areas divided only by sliding screens, or strategically-placed cupboards.

The changing styles in school designs have been influenced by economic, social and political pressures. Many teachers believe that these have outweighed educational considerations which might have influenced the architects.

The effects of building design

Open plan designs do, in some respects, work well for those who believe that education should be child-centred, co-operative etc. Nevertheless, teachers frequently complain that they are not consulted about the plans of the buildings in which they have to work. On the other hand, teachers themselves have widely differing attitudes to teaching methods, and frequently move jobs, so that catering for particular teachers is not a very practical approach to the problem of school design.

Teachers must consider the physical constraints which will affect the way they teach. Team teaching, for example, is likely to be impossible in classrooms which are filled to capacity with 30 children and linked only by a corridor. However, if one classroom is linked to a hall which is not always used for PE, or music sessions etc, some form of co-operative teaching can probably be organised.

Open plan schools are not suitable for separate class teaching unless every class is working in its own area at the same time. Even then, screens which are relatively sound-proof are needed to separate the open areas.

Chapter Six

Career development

Most teachers, male and female, enter the teaching profession with the idea of developing a career. Women who expect to take some time away from the classroom in order to have their own families, often anticipate returning and continuing their career.

There are many factors involved in developing a satisfactory career.

Of these, the first year of service is one of the most significant. All teachers remember their first year in teaching — some because of its importance as a probationary year, others because it was their first year as a bona fide member of staff in a school.

It is possible that under new proposals for teacher training the probationary year may disappear. At present, however, it remains a significant feature in that training.

The probationary year

The probationary year is significant in a formal way as it is used to assess a teacher's competence. Informally, it should be seen as a time when extra help and advice is available to the newly qualified teacher and when lasting friendships and professional relationships are born. For every probationary teacher, there are triumphs to be savoured, and difficulities to be overcome, just as there are for more experienced teachers.

There has been concern for a number of years about the organisation of the probationary year, and some initiatives have been undertaken to try and improve its format. These initiatives have, however, been piecemeal, and varied from one LEA to another, and even from school to school. Where progress has been made towards developing structured policies to help probationary teachers, economic restraints have often led to their curtailment.

A few teachers believe that money spent on probationers is wasted, but most appreciate that a better, more structured approach to probation would not only benefit the new teacher, but also improve the teaching profession as a whole. It is interesting to realise, for example, that PGCE courses, with their intensive single year of training, were originally only acceptable because the probationary year was expected to add a further, strong component to the training. Present LEA practices frequently do not offer any further training. The HMI document, *The New Teacher in School* (HMSO 1982) noted that almost 30 per cent of their sample of primary schools provided a less than satisfactory environment for new teachers. A good school atmosphere is not, in itself, enough to support a probationary teacher. HMI reported that the best ways of supporting the probationary teacher included releasing experienced teachers for one or two hours per week to work with new teachers, and the specific use of senior staff to advise in their particular areas of responsibility.

In the classroom the main problems which new teachers have to face are those of organisation and discipline. In many cases, these are made worse by the need to cater for wide ranges of ability. To help the probationer cope in the early stages with their problems, induction schemes should ensure that:

- The probationer's work load is lighter than that of experienced teachers.
- Clear information is provided about school procedures and policies.
- Counselling is available on matters concerning the school, classroom and local authority. This should include advice on organisation, opportunities to watch experienced colleagues at work, and time to discuss matters of importance with people outside the school.
- Probationers in the same area have regular meetings together.
- At least one experienced member of staff keeps an eye on the probationer.

These items can place heavy burdens on schools, but even the most self-sufficient newcomer will benefit from a programme of this kind. If the probationary year does become defunct, some system of supporting new entrants to the profession will have to be devised.

Suggestions for probationary teachers:

- Become familiar with the resources of the school and the LEA, some of which may be held at the local teachers' centre. Don't forget the human resources of head and other staff in the school, and also any local authority officers who may be detailed to help new teachers.
- If contact between local probationers is not organised initially by the LEA, the newcomers themselves ought to arrange some get-togethers.
- Seek advice, and do not feel that the inability to cope with problems in teaching amounts to failure. No matter how competent other teachers appear to be, they too have difficulties, and will have experienced other difficulties in the past. Use their experience to help cope with problems.
- Do not forget that teaching is an enjoyable experience, and that a real comradeship exists in staffrooms. Take advantage of this comradeship.

Though probationers should attend some INSET courses, it is not a good idea to attend too many. Teaching practice experience will have left new teachers in no doubt about how tiring teaching can be, but the probationary year will be their first experience of a complete year in the classroom. A small number of useful INSET courses will invigorate and refresh the teacher, but a large number of boring and unhelpful courses can have the opposite effect. The so called 'Baker days' ought to provide a basis for the new teachers' in-service training.

At the end of the probationary year, new teachers need to consider the career pattern they expect to follow, and begin to think of the best way in-service courses can be used to develop their career.

In-service training

Teachers' ambitions vary enormously. From the ranks of newly-trained teachers will eventually come educational psychologists, headteachers, local authority inspectors, HMIs, teacher trainers etc. Some teachers simply, and laudably, want to become as good as possible at being classroom teachers. Whatever their eventual achievements, however, most teachers who fulfil their ambitions will have gained some benefit from in-service training.

At the beginning of their careers, this training is similar for all teachers. Virtually all teachers in the first years of their careers attend courses on curriculum development, rather than, for example, the specialist courses in management techniques designed for headteachers, or educational psychology courses for aspiring psychologists.

The variety of courses

Those responsible for working out the content of courses should bear in mind the future needs of the teaching profession. Society and its needs are changing so quickly that teachers have to come to grips with new and unfamiliar skills, and at the same time have to develop their own teaching skills. Short courses, organised under GRIST arrangements with local needs in mind provide good opportunities to learn these skills and supplement the long courses organised by the education departments of universities, polytechnics, and other institutions of higher education. Some categories of courses are designated by the Secretary of State as national priorities while others are designated by a local authority as having local priority. Since the former courses attract a 70 per cent government grant, and the latter a 50 per cent grant, the number of courses available in particular curriculum areas is going to be affected by the Secretary of State's perceptions of teachers' needs.

What I have said about probationers attending in-service courses applies equally to experienced teachers attending such courses. Yet there can be no doubt that a good in-service programme, set up for school staff under the GRIST arrangements, can be invaluable. Such courses are, however, not always used appropriately.

I remember going on a residential course at which an eminent speaker was lecturing about the implications of the technological revolution for the primary school curriculum. The guest had to leave straight after the speech, leaving the subsequent discussion in the hands of a local authority adviser. This hapless gentleman announced an adjournment for tea, followed by a group discussion on how much swimming and spelling ought to be in the primary curriculum. It was certainly not the best moment to introduce such mundane, though admittedly important, subjects.

Many local authorities use a rolling course system. For example, in computer education, some authorities have tried to ensure that courses run continuously. Schools are urged to have at least one member of staff who can teach others in their school the rudiments of using computers in the classroom. The employment of curriculum leaders has helped here, and this type of development has often led the way for school-based in-service training.

Specialist courses

Courses in subjects such as CDT, science and maths, where specialist teachers are in short supply, have become increasingly popular. They attract interested teachers, and funding. Teachers in some local authorities are being seconded into teams to develop CDT in primary schools, run courses, and provide support and advice for their colleagues. Primary teachers with particular expertise in maths provide a similar service.

In addition to the benefits teachers gain, those who attend the courses increase their prospects of moving into teacher training or the advisory services.

Initial Training Courses
Another way in which teachers can gain some insight into teacher training is through ITINSET (initial training linked to in-service training). Originated at the University of Leicester School of Education, it is now part of the initial training programme for teachers at many other establishments, though clearly it is only available to schools in the vicinity of such institutions. Small groups of students work on a project in the classroom in co-operation with class teachers and tutors. The project which a team undertakes is initiated by the teacher, but all members of the team are equal participants. One objective of ITINSET is to allow self-evaluation and development through the collective learning experience. Classroom practice is analysed, theory applied, and the curriculum evaluated and developed.

For teachers interested in finding out about career development in teacher training, most training institutions have schemes which involve practising teachers in that training. This usually means that a teacher is seconded as a lecturer, under the title of associate, or teacher tutor. Details are available from the institutions, though under the GRIST arrangements, these positions are more restricted than they used to be.

Teachers who hope to become head-teachers need to consider training for management.

Training for management

A constant and valid criticism of the career structure within our education system is that the best classroom teachers are promoted to roles outside the classroom. However, good teachers do not necessarily make good heads. The revised career structure of 1987 does little to persuade good teachers to stay in the classroom, and those who are promoted have to be trained in management techniques.

Fortunately, for headteachers and aspiring headteachers, there have been significant developments in management training over the past decade. Though these have been prompted partly by the perceived improvements in management training in industry and commerce, some teachers are wary of applying the theory of industrial management to the organisation of schools. However, it is almost certain that future headteachers will be expected to gain more of the type of management expertise which business managers have.

Many first and higher degree courses for serving teachers include aspects of management, and there are also excellent one term management courses and basic three week courses, that have been supported by the Training Grants Scheme. These enable heads and deputies to get together to discuss school management issues.

Skills in leadership, communication, delegation, motivation and decision making are examined; these are central to management practices in schools, just as they are in business, commerce and industry. Even for heads of small schools, management training is essential. Those teachers who hope eventually to run their own school are well advised to attend an appropriate course before applying for headships.

One of the most important tasks of a headteacher is being involved in staff appraisal. Although staff appraisal may not be directly linked to the promotion of teachers, it has a strong role to play in career development. Those teachers looking for promotion need to consider the implications of appraisal very carefully.

Appraisal

The 1985 government White Paper *Better Schools* advocated regular and formal appraisal of teachers so that local education authorities could assist in the professional development of teachers.

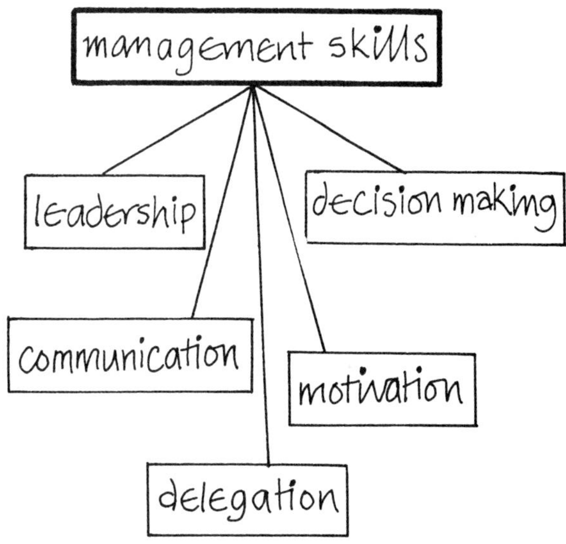

The Education Act of 1986 gave the Secretary of State the power to impose a framework for appraisal if necessary.

Broadly speaking, there are two approaches to the notion of appraising staff who work in the education service.

First, there is the idea that appraisal ought to be carried out to improve the quality of an individual teacher's work, helping to increase job satisfaction, and helping to identify in-service needs. The other view is that appraisal ought to be an integral part of the assessment of a teacher's suitability for promotion and salary increases. In one sense, therefore, it is seen as being linked to punitive procedures, and is certainly seen as a means of making the education system more cost-effective.

Most teachers are not opposed to

appraisal in some form. Indeed there is general agreement on several fundamental points:

- Appraisal should not be confined to the classroom teacher.
- The process ought to include an element of self-appraisal.
- Classroom observation and interviews at appropriate times are integral parts of appraisal.
- Appraisal ought to be a continuous process.

It is easy to identify some of the difficulties which might arise if the underlying philosophy links appraisal to promotion. Most obviously, appraisal could be used to compare the performance of teachers, rather than a means of improving the teaching of an individual.

Difficulties of appraisal

Although the data gathered from appraisal may not initially be intended to be comparative material for assessment, it could be seen by future administrators as a cost-effective way of determining a teacher's suitability for promotion. If this does happen, teachers could reasonably ask how comparisons could be made between teachers teaching different age groups, or teaching in schools with differing approaches to organisation, or in schools with different resource levels.

What facility would there be for the comparison to take account of the difference in teaching in various catchment areas, and how can appraisal carried out by different headteachers be compared?

Clearly these concerns are significant for teachers wanting promotion, and will influence the morale of the teaching force as a whole. Appraisal is certain to make a real impact on the career development of ambitious teachers.

Chapter Seven

Conclusion

In the first chapter, I suggested that teachers need to look closely at their own teaching, in order to improve. If teaching practices are to improve, good evaluation techniques are necessary. Throughout the book, I have emphasised evaluation and the importance of building good relationships as two of the most significant factors in developing effective primary school teaching.

While evaluation is undoubtedly carried out by most teachers on an individual basis, it is certain to become part of an appraisal process in school and the local authority. In such situations, good relationships with colleagues throughout the education service are essential.

Good relationships are founded in the pride of being a member of a well-respected profession, in confidence in the quality of education offered by an LEA and in the self-esteem that comes from being a teacher contributing to the work of a particular school.

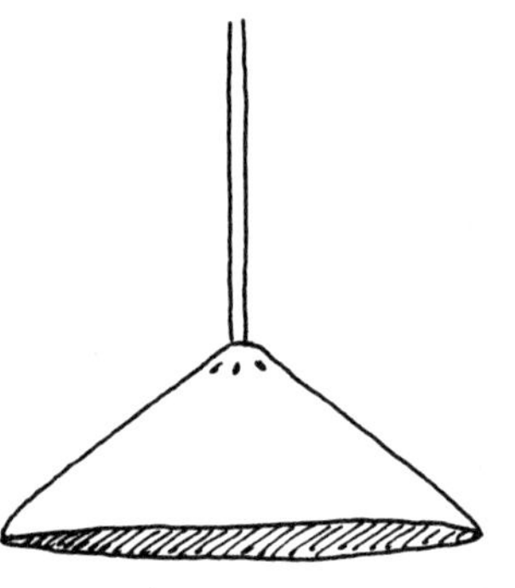

Until recently, the comparative autonomy of the teaching profession as a whole, with individual teachers, school staffs, and local authorities being responsible for making their own decisions at certain levels, was a major factor in keeping teachers' morale high, in keeping relationships good, and hence in making the possibility of incisive evaluation a reality. Unfortunately, however, classroom teachers, headteachers, and LEAs are gradually losing their autonomous power.

Government policy

Although this book is mainly concerned with the practicalities of teaching, I have made frequent references to the influence of government policy on education, and its consequent influence on teachers' jobs.

As a result of a political initiative, the debate about a national curriculum was regenerated in 1987 and has led to the proposals in the Education Reform Bill (see Chapter 4).

An earlier act (1986) was seen by government ministers as a means of giving parents more say in the running of schools, of increasing control over the curriculum, and of raising teaching standards. It altered the composition of schools' governing bodies, affected the provision of INSET (see Chapter 6) and gave the Secretary of State the power to dictate a framework for the appraisal of teachers (also discussed in Chapter 6).

If the 1986 Act and the Education Reform Bill prove to be simply the start of an accelerating process of removing teacher autonomy, they could become major factors in reducing teachers' morale. This will in turn sour relationships within the education service and will affect the continuation and development of constructive evaluative procedures.

Teachers, however, have the interests of their pupils at heart, and in spite of difficulties, will no doubt continue to seek ways of improving their teaching. I hope that the suggestions and information in this volume will contribute in some measure to that improvement.

Appendix

References

Clark E and Clark H (1977) *Psychology and Language* Harcourt Brace Jovanovich
Bruner J (1966) *Towards a Theory of Instruction* Norton
Bryant P E (1975) *Perception and Understanding in Young Children* Methuen
Donaldson M (1978) *Children's Minds* Fontana
Ennever L and Harlen W (1972) *With Objectives in Mind* MacDonald
HMSO 15 (1982) *The New Teacher in School, Matters for Discussion*
HMSO (1983) *Teaching Quality*
HMSO (1985) *Better Schools*
Houlton D (1986) *Cultural Diversity in the Primary School* Batsford
DES (1987) *National Curriculum 5-16: A Consultation Document*
Nuffield Maths Project (1967-74) Murray
Powell J (1985) *The Teacher's Craft* SCRE Publications
Wells G (1985) *Language, Learning and Education* NFER
DES (1988) *National Curriculum: Task Group on Assessment and Testing — A Report*
Piaget J — probably the best way to begin considering Piaget's work is to see the summary in Donaldson M, noted above.

Index

D

E

F

G

H

I

Q

R

S

T

Other Scholastic Books

Bright Ideas
The *Bright Ideas* books provide a wealth of resources for busy primary school teachers. There are now more than 20 titles published, providing clearly explained and illustrated ideas on topics ranging from *Writing* and *Maths Activities* to *Assemblies* and *Christmas Art and Craft*. Each book contains material which can be photocopied for use in the classroom.

Teacher Handbooks
The *Teacher Handbooks* give an overview of the latest research in primary education, and show how it can be put into practice in the classroom. Covering all the core areas of the curriculum, the *Teacher Handbooks* are indispensable to the new teacher as a source of information and useful to the experienced teacher as a quick reference guide.

Management Books
The *Management Books* are designed to help teachers to organise their time, classroom and teaching more efficiently. The books deal with topical issues, such as *Parents and Schools* and organising and planning *Project Teaching*, and are written by authors with lots of practical advice and experiences to share.

International Bookshelf
The *International Bookshelf* is a selection of informative education books available in the UK exclusively through Scholastic. Truly representative of international thinking these books are classics in their own field.

Big Books
Big Books are poster-sized books, aimed at five- to nine-year-olds, which have been specially designed so that a group of children can share a book with an adult and still have that feeling of togetherness which is so important for early readers who are building up confidence. Included in each pack is a giant-sized book, six smaller books for individual reading and teacher notes.

006149

LINKED